Survivors of Enemy Action

Other Books by Bernard Edwards

Masters Next to God
They Sank the Red Dragon
The Fighting Tramps
The Grey Widow-Maker
Blood and Bushido
SOS – Men Against the Sea
Salvo!
*Attack and Sink**
*Dönitz and the Wolf Packs**
Return of the Coffin Ships
*Beware Raiders!**
*The Road to Russia**
*The Quiet Heroes**
*The Twilight of the U-boats**
Beware the Grey Widow-Maker
*Death in the Doldrums**
*Japan's Blitzkrieg**
*War of the U-boats**
*Royal Navy Versus the Slave Trade**
*The Cruel Sea Retold**
*War Under the Red Ensign 1914–1918**
*The Wolf Packs Gather**
*Convoy Will Scatter**
*The Decoys**
*U-boats Beyond Biscay**
*Churchill's Thin Grey Line**
*From Hunter to Hunted**
*Running the Gauntlet**

* Denotes titles in print with Pen & Sword Books

Survivors of Enemy Action

Experiences of Merchant Seamen 1939–1945

Bernard Edwards

Pen & Sword
MARITIME

First published in Great Britain in 2023 by
Pen & Sword Maritime
An imprint of Pen & Sword Books Limited
Yorkshire – Philadelphia

ISBN 978 1 39904 220 8

A CIP catalogue record for this book is
available from the British Library

Typeset by Mac Style
Printed in the UK by CPI Group (UK) Ltd, Croydon, CR0 4YY.

Pen & Sword Books Limited incorporates the imprints of After the
Battle, Atlas, Archaeology, Aviation, Discovery, Family History,
Fiction, History, Maritime, Military, Military Classics, Politics,
Select, Transport, True Crime, Air World, Frontline Publishing,
Leo Cooper, Remember When, Seaforth Publishing, The Praetorian
Press, Wharncliffe Local History, Wharncliffe Transport,
Wharncliffe True Crime and White Owl.

For a complete list of Pen & Sword titles please contact

PEN & SWORD BOOKS LIMITED
47 Church Street, Barnsley, South Yorkshire, S70 2AS, England
E-mail: enquiries@pen-and-sword.co.uk
Website: www.pen-and-sword.co.uk
or
PEN AND SWORD BOOKS
1950 Lawrence Rd, Havertown, PA 19083, USA
E-mail: Uspen-and-sword@casematepublishers.com
Website: www.penandswordbooks.com

This one is for 'Dai bach'. May he grow up in a world at peace.

> Listen, while I tell you tales of the sea,
> Of tumbling waves and whistling winds,
> And all things tight and free.
>
> Of the thundering guns in a world at war,
> When the adrenaline was all aroar.
>
> Of long, lazy days in tropic seas,
> With cotton-wool clouds and cooling rains,
> And the sky at night alight
> With ten thousand twinkling stars.
>
> And I'll tell you tales of ports afar
> From old Cape Town to Singapore,
> And south again to Sydney's shore.
> Oh, what wondrous sights we did see.

Bernard Edwards 2022

Contents

Author's Note

In the war years of 1939–45, fortunate indeed was the British merchant seaman who completed an ocean passage without being on the receiving end of an enemy torpedo, shell or bomb, or negotiated the approaches to a strange port without being blown up by an underwater mine. Yet those who manned the ships in those perilous days took it all in their stride. They fought against unbelievable odds, but they were never 'heat-of-the-moment' heroes. With the exception of a very small minority who mistakenly thought the sea was a safe hiding place for the duration, they were professionals, following a career they would have chosen come war or peace. 'Stoical' is a good word to describe them.

The price those men paid for this devotion to career was heavy: 2,535 ships sunk, 36,749 of all ranks lost – a higher proportional casualty rate than any of the Armed Services except Bomber Command. Yet, sadly, I write having just watched the annual Armistice Day service at the Cenotaph in London where the men of Britain's Merchant Navy were apparently invisible, rating only one brief mention by the commentator, and that *en passant*. 'Forgotten' is another word that springs to mind.

On the lighter side, there were the ones who got away – the survivors. This book, compiled mainly from experiences related to the author first-hand, supplemented by the retelling of reports lodged at The National Archives, Kew, tells their story.

Chapter One

The Return of the Q-ship

The Q-ship was initially used by the Royal Navy in the First World War. Suitable merchant ships were taken up, armed with concealed weapons, and sent out to deal with unsuspecting German U-boats. The plan met with moderate success, and when war broke out again in 1939, a decision was made to bring back the Q-ships.

One of the first to be commissioned was HMS *Willamette Valley*. A motor vessel of 4,724 tons gross, she was built on the Clyde in 1928 as the *West Lynn* for the Reardon Smith Line of Cardiff, who renamed her *Willamette Valley* in 1931. On 17 September 1939, she was requisitioned by the Royal Navy and taken to Chatham, where she was equipped with nine 4-inch guns, a 12-pounder, and four 21-inch torpedo tubes, all concealed by shutters. In addition, she was fitted with ASDIC and carried 100 depth charges, all of which combined to make HMS *Willamette Valley* a formidable submarine hunter, with the outward appearance of a run-of-the-mill tramp. She was in the charge of Lieutenant Commander Robert Ryder, who in March 1942 won the Victoria Cross while leading the commando raid on the dry dock at Saint-Nazaire.

Cornelius Blake was a radio officer aboard the *Willamette Valley*.

I started off at sea as a cabin boy on the *Pardo*, belonging to the Royal Mail Line. We made exactly the same route as Darwin, as far down as Bahia Blanca, Deseado and through the Magellan Straits. In 1931, on my third trip to sea, I fell down the hold of a ship called the *Salado*, which belonged to the Argentine

Railway Company. I broke both legs and was three years in the Royal Gwent [Royal Gwent Hospital, Newport]. When I came out, I decided to quit Newport. My people kept the Welcome Home in Dolphin Street. For a short while, I went as a cadet with my twin brother on a ship called the *Helmstrath*, owned by the Strath Steamship Company. Downs were the agents in Cardiff. After the first voyage, I landed back in hospital again. I lost a lot of sea time, but I was determined not to go back to sea in the forecastle, so I went to London and took a radio ticket. That was 1936. I then went back to my first company, Royal Mail, as a radio officer. Later, I was in the *Faraday* on cable laying.

When war broke out in 1939, I came back home on the *Highland Princess* and was told to go on leave. The money was still coming through but I didn't know what was happening. Then Siemens of London sent for me. The next thing I knew, I had been shanghaied into the Navy and ended up in Chatham Barracks. I was given the rank of sub lieutenant (special duties).

I spent three months in the barracks, and then I was directed to this wreck of a ship in Chatham Dockyard. We were told that the ship was No. 2015, but she was really the *Willamette Valley*, belonging to Smith's of Cardiff. I said to the electrician, Quince, who was with me, 'What's that thing?' 'Oh,' he said, 'she's probably going to be used as a block ship.' We went aboard and had a good look around. When we got back to our billets, Quince said, 'I don't like it.' I said, 'It's damn stupid. Timber in the holds. And she's got diesel tanks. What happens if she's hit? Everything will be soaked in oil.' We were not happy.

I went on board the *Willamette Valley* and was greeted by Commander Ryder, who told me it was a Q-ship and a volunteer job. Some managed to worm their way out of it. I suppose I was young and inexperienced – and too patriotic. Anyway, I didn't have the guts to refuse, so I stayed with her. The crew were a mixture of Royal Navy, Royal Naval Reserve and Merchant Navy, all in uniform and under naval discipline. There were 150 on board. The ratings slept in hammocks in the tween decks, where it was wet and cold. The water came through the gun shutters. The first and second radio officers had separate cabins, but I was in a double cabin. She was very heavily armed for a ship of her type, but not fast enough or strong enough. She had four 4.7-inch guns, torpedo tubes and depth charge throwers. We were fated not to use any of them.

We left Chatham as HMS *Edgehill*. First, we went down to the Western Approaches to try to trace the *Altmark*. We had no luck with that and cruised up and down off the Azores. There were two German Q-ships in port. We could see one of them was registered in Hamburg and the crew were over the stern removing the port of registry. We withdrew over the horizon with the object of ambushing her when she came out. My God, I was glad we didn't get near her. She was doing 25–26 knots, and all we could do was 10. She had 6-inch guns on hydraulic lifts, and when the guns came up the shutters automatically dropped open ready to fire. No doubt, she could have blown us to smithereens. But it didn't come to that. We were steaming into a headwind and she was out of range before we could get near her. When I think back on it, the whole thing was ridiculous. We wouldn't have stood a chance.

Then we proceeded to Bermuda and the South Atlantic to see if we could locate the raider, but it was no use. We spent three months chasing up and down. On our way back across the Atlantic we ran into heavy weather and damaged our gun shutters, so we had to make for Gib. Unlike the German ones, which were electrically controlled, our shutters had hand chains for economy. The Germans didn't believe in cheeseparing on their raiders, but the British Government did.

When we were on our way into Gibraltar harbour, a Spanish tug came out from Algeciras. I happened to be standing on the bridge at the time and the tug gave us a hell of a thump. I looked over the side and saw she had hit us right on top of the shutters. The shutter fell down and you could plainly see the gun behind. I never did trust those Spaniards. At the time, we were disguised as a fleet auxiliary. I think the name was *Edlington Court*. We had so many changes of disguise that I could never remember which we were supposed to be.

We were in Gib when France fell. I saw one of the Usk boats in port and went on board. I met a fireman called O'Day, from Newport. He lost his life shortly afterwards. We had been in Gib about a week or ten days when we suddenly got a signal from the Admiralty to proceed to the Bay of Biscay, where there was submarine activity. Our orders were (1) to engage and sink enemy submarines and (2) to land a party ashore to investigate the possibility of future landing on the French coast. When we left Gib, we were disguised as a Greek. We had spent three days changing funnels, painting the ship, putting a Greek flag on the hull, etc.

After two and a half days steaming from Gib, we arrived off Saint-Nazaire. I remember Number One, Lieutenant Seymour, saying to the company in the wardroom, 'No sub activity tonight, Gentlemen. Too many whitecaps.' At about eleven o'clock I went below for supper. I was due on the 12–4 watch. Then I went down to check the batteries. The surgeon lieutenant, a charming man called Wallace, who had been in Union Castle, sat down with me and we talked. We were both a bit fed up, as we had been running round in circles in the Atlantic for so long. Wallace said, 'I've had just about enough of this. I was a damn fool to join up. All this ruddy braid nonsense. I've been worked to death and sick to death for three months. If only we had a torpedo in the bows, so we could go home for repairs. He went down with the ship.

I got up to the radio room just on midnight to relieve my opposite number. Just then, there was one hell of a bang and the place collapsed around us. Then the alarm bells started ringing. My action station was on No. 2 gun on the starboard side. In order to get there I had to go through the saloon and down a hatch controlled by electricity. It was a nasty business. You pressed a button and the hatch flew open, and you climbed down to what had previously been the tween decks. There was only room for one at a time to go down. I got to the pantry, where this hatch was hidden, and I had just pressed the button to open it when there was another bang. The gundeck was splattered in blood and mess and I was blown across the saloon.

My next duty, when I picked myself up, was to take part in a 'panic party'. We were to leave the ship in a lifeboat to give the impression she was being abandoned. The idea was that the U-boat would then surface, the gun shutters would be raised and the 4.7s would open fire, sinking the sub. That was the theory, anyway. Of course, everything went wrong. The timber in the holds went on fire, as I had feared it would do. One RNVR lieutenant had been killed. Martin was his name – poor devil. He was an ex-Guards officer; 6-foot 2 and so fussy, but an awfully nice bloke. Why the hell he joined the Navy I don't know. Probably because he used to go yachting with Commander Ryder.

When we went to launch the boat, we, being Merchant Navy, were the only ones who knew how to handle the old-fashioned davits and falls. We got the boat swung out but I found one of the hooks was moused. I shouted for a knife, but there wasn't one seaman with a knife on him. I put my hand in my pocket – I remember the feeling so well, even after forty-eight years – and I found a small pocketknife I used to sharpen my pencils in the radio room. I cut the mousing and freed the falls. The next thing, we went down with a hell of a bump. Half the crew were pitched into the water, but we picked them up and rowed away from the ship, for we thought we had seen the sub surfacing. It was a moonlit night and the visibility was deceiving. There was also a strong wind blowing and there were a lot of whitecaps in the water. What looked like a sub – and we didn't realise this until sometime afterwards – was actually the starboard lifeboat. They also mistook us for the sub, and thinking they would be caught in the crossfire between the ship and the enemy, they backed water and went around the starboard side of the ship out of the way. The next torpedo went right through the boat as she was trying to get alongside.

Obviously, we had walked into a trap, set up by the information given by the Spanish tug in Gib. There must have been at least three submarines and they must have known what we were. When this torpedo went through the ship, it really did the damage. After it hit the starboard panic party boat, it went through the engine room and hit the ammunition locker. The whole ruddy lot went up like a box of matches. She just disintegrated. The funnel went up, the masts went up and everybody went up. Those below decks wouldn't have had a snowball's chance in hell of getting out. We rowed back towards the burning wreck but the only one we picked up was the 1st radio officer, Pearson. He was completely exhausted and covered in oil. How he got out still puzzles me. The radio gear was in the worst possible place, right forward under the forecastle head. There was only one way in or out, and that was through a heavy steel door that was intended to deaden the noise of the guns. How he got that door open with the ship listing, I'll never understand.

The sea was now so rough that further attempts at rescue were hopeless. Men drowned before our eyes or drifted out of sight and perished. Next day, we sighted a raft with eleven men on board. When we got them into the boat they said there had been more than thirty on the raft originally, but most of them had been washed off by rough seas during the night.

We were adrift for four days, during which time we saw a searching aircraft and a convoy, but both failed to see our distress signals. By this time, most of us were in a sorry state due to exposure. Our lips were so dry and cracked it was almost impossible to suck the hard lifeboat biscuits. Even drinking the quarter of a dipper of water proved an effort. Our bodies were covered in salt-water blisters, each the size of a penny.

It was noon on the fifth day when we sighted the trawler. She was flying the German flag over the French Tricolour and we were very apprehensive about approaching her. We took a show of hands on it, but we were all in such a state by now that there could be only one result. We rigged the lugsail and sailed towards the trawler, which seemed to be hauling her nets. She was the *Dombien* and fortunately for us, the skipper was pro-British and there were no Germans on board. I suppose they took a chance on rescuing us, as there were thirty of us in the boat and we outnumbered them. But they treated us well and agreed to take us to England, in return for a promise that they would not be interned. They were worried about reprisals being taken against their families. The senior survivor, Sub Lieutenant Tilley, gave this assurance, but after they had landed us in Penzance, the Admiralty seized their boat.

After that, I was torpedoed twice and bombed three times. I lost the sight of my left eye when I was torpedoed off New Orleans in a Norwegian fleet auxiliary tanker. I met Lieutenant Pembury in 1941, when I was serving in one of Smith's again. He told me that the ramming by the Spanish tug in Gib had been quite deliberate and designed to expose our guns. The presence of the subs in the Bay had also been a trick to lure us out and put paid to us. Commander Ryder was in on the Saint-Nazaire business and tried to take me with him. But the doctor said, 'He can't see properly, and he can't walk properly,' which was true.

I left the Navy in 1944 and went with P & A Campbell's for twelve months. Then I went teaching. I still remember vividly the horror of that first action of the war, the sinking of the *Willamette Valley*, Reardon Smith's raider that never fired a shot in anger.

When Con Blake told me his story, he was living alone, an ageing, chain-smoking pensioner thoroughly disillusioned with life, and with nothing to show for the great sacrifices he had made for his country. In common with so many of his fellow merchant seamen, he died unrecognised.

Chapter Two

Eastbound Convoy, September 1940

In the late summer of 1940, Britain faced the might of Hitler's war machine alone, and was dependent on the arsenals and granaries of the Americas for her survival. This involved an almost continuous chain of supply convoys crossing the Atlantic under the protection of the British and Canadian navies, who, after a year of constant activity and heavy losses, were running short of ocean escorts.

As a last resort, armed merchant cruisers, ex-passenger liners, armed and manned by reservists, were being pressed into service. But there were never enough of these ships, and as a compromise, they were used to cover convoys in mid-ocean only. When the demand was great, which was often, they were forced to leave the convoy before the destroyer escorts took over, leaving the merchantmen to look to their own defence. This was so with the eastbound HX 72.

Stanley Walton was a deck apprentice in the old coal burner *Selvistan*.

So far as I remember, we sailed from Curtis Bay, Baltimore, with a full cargo of scrap metal for Halifax, where degaussing cables were installed, and proceeded to Sydney, Cape Breton, for bunkers, going alongside a coal staith for about eight hours, then off to the anchorage to await the convoy sailing date. We sailed in convoy with a couple of small Canadian Navy escorts who left us when we joined up with the other section from Halifax, with *Jervis Bay* as Ocean Escort. She was a fine-looking vessel and steamed in the middle of the convoy. At that time, the weather I think was fair as we kept daylight lookout in a barrel on the foremast crosstrees and at night on the fo'c'sle head, until the weather changed and lookout was from the monkey island. I was in a watch with two old ABs, ex-RN. The watch system was four on, four off, four on then eight off, then field day of four hours, etc., during which time the lookout, wheel and standby duties were shared by the three of us and those in the other two watches. We carried a bosun, ex-Head Line apprentice named, I think, Wills from Whitley Bay, and an old Norwegian carpenter, who were day workers, and that was the deck crowd. I was also sight setter on the old low-angle gun mounted on the poop, as we only had an ex-RN (ret'd) leading hand gunlayer. The rest of the gun's crew were mainly from the deck and catering departments, Second Mate George Miles being the gunnery officer, and I think Muloholland, the chief steward, was the gun trainer, and Bulmore, my mate, was a tray or breech worker. *Selvistan* was a single-decker, coal-burning, ice box ship, a poor feeder with spartan accommodation. The crew lived forward, firemen on the port side, deck crowd on the starboard side of the fo'c'sle, each side being equipped with a small coal-burning bogey stove for heat in the open sleeping quarters. There was a separate mess room and primitive toilet on each side. The chart room was on the lower bridge forward of the chief officer's cabin, which also opened onto the deck. Our 6' x 6' room was on the port side amidships and opened out onto the deck. It contained two bunks with lumpy flock mattresses, a 3-foot settee, a chest, an oil lamp, a 40 watt light bulb in the centre of the wooden deckhead that leaked, and a ventilator that was located between the jolly boat and the Old Man's room bulkhead on the lower bridge above, as well as a converted washbasin stand that served as our food locker, containing condensed milk, sugar, coffee, tea, jam and bread. The cook wasn't the best; the daily 1lb loaf had a crust on each end and a lump of 'sog' in the middle, and the tinned Irish butter that we used to swop with the West African firemen for cheese or jam – generally apple or damson – was soft and very salty/rancid and quite strong-smelling. There was no table; meals were consumed sitting on the settee with the enamel metal kits on your knee, with the rod and chain groaning and clanking overhead. The radio 'shack' was on the after end of the boat deck, which was equipped with radial davits and a wooden lifeboat on each side.

Jervis Bay left the convoy, and the first night we were without an escort. I recall being on the 8–12 second wheel (10 to 12), and when the *Invershannon* was hit at 0100 hours, there was a rain squall over the convoy. We stood by the 4-inch gun for a few hours before we were stood down and joined the rest of the off-watch crew squatted on the boat deck until daylight, when we resumed our normal duties until nightfall, when we had a repeat performance.

We were on passage for, I think it was twenty-one days, and we had to bunker at Greenock to make the trip, north about, to Middlesbrough as an independent ship. We almost stood still punching the tide through the Pentland Firth; flat out and with a strong stern wind, we could only make 9 knots. In spite of her shortcomings, she was quite a happy ship, even though the captain wasn't exactly 'Mr Geneality'. He was a Whitby man; I was at Nellist's Nautical School, Newcastle, for second mates, with his son.

No doubt, you have all the info pertaining to the composition of the convoy etc. It was quite an adventure for a 15-year-old.

I left the ship in November and became an indentured apprentice with B.J. Sutherland & Co. Ltd. of Newcastle, on their m.v. *Sutherland*; I thought I'd joined the *Queen Mary* – good accommodation, excellent food, meals in the saloon, study periods at sea from 3 to 5, etc. I stayed in the ship until March 1945, the last year as third mate.

Chapter Three

Raider at Large

German U-boats were particularly active on the North Atlantic convoy routes in the autumn of 1940, sinking seventy-two Allied merchantmen in October alone, but the real menace was yet to come.

On 31 October 1940, the Deutschland-class heavy cruiser *Admiral Scheer* slipped through the Denmark Strait into the Atlantic undetected by Allied patrols. The 28-knot cruiser, armed with six 11-inch guns in triple turrets, eight 5.9s in single turrets and eight 21-inch torpedo tubes, was on her first offensive patrol of the Second World War. Her primary aim was to seek out Allied convoys, which were known to be weakly defended at that time, and cause as much chaos as possible before the heavy units of the Royal Navy caught up with her.

Just forty-eight hours before the *Admiral Scheer* emerged into the North Atlantic, Convoy HX 84 sailed eastbound from Halifax, Nova Scotia. Consisting of thirty-seven heavily laden merchantmen, HX 84 was escorted by the armed merchant cruiser HMS *Jervis Bay*, an ex-passenger liner armed with eight 1914–18 vintage 6-inch guns firing over open sights. HX 84 and the *Admiral Scheer* were on converging courses.

The confrontation, when it occurred on the evening of 5 November, was brutal and bloody. The *Admiral Scheer*'s 11-inch guns made short work of the *Jervis Bay*, turning her into a blazing wreck with a few well-aimed salvoes. The convoy scattered, but not before the German guns had sent another five ships to the bottom.

Captain Fellingham, who was sailing as third officer in one of the ships that got away, remembers:

I had joined the *Trefusis* – a First World War standard 'three island' type trampship of 5,299grt, built at Sunderland in 1918 – as third mate in February 1939, and she was to be my home for the next twenty-two months. Although she was slow and not very comfortable, she was my first berth as an officer after getting my second mate's ticket and I was quite content in her. However, after the start of the Second World War on 3 September 1939, it soon became apparent that she had a habit of living dangerously, as almost every convoy in which she sailed was attacked by submarines, planes or E-boats, or sustained loss due to mines. In addition, almost every UK port we entered suffered an air raid while we were there. By the autumn of 1940, we hadn't encountered an attack by a surface warship, but that was about to change. *Trefusis* had led a charmed life while I was in her, but her luck finally ran out on 5 March 1943, when she was sunk by a torpedo.

After discharging a cargo of Anson training aeroplanes and spare parts at Montreal, we loaded a consignment of steel bars overstowed with a quantity of dressed timber, including an 8ft high deck cargo, all destined for Hull. We left Montreal on 25 October 1940, and arrived at Sydney, Cape Breton, on the 28th to await convoy. We sailed from Sydney on 29 October and joined the Halifax section of Convoy HX 84 later that day. The *Trefusis* was allocated the position of last ship in column 4, and by dusk on the 29th, Convoy HX 84, consisting of thirty-seven merchant ships and our escort, AMC *Jervis Bay*, had formed up and set a north-easterly course for the UK. For the next seven days, life was as uneventful as is possible in a wartime convoy. The weather was reasonable for the time of year and the convoy made a speed of about 8 knots on a course of N52E.

On the morning of 5 November 1940, I took my usual 8–12 bridge watch, taking morning longitude by chronometer sights of brief shots of the sun appearing through a generally overcast sky. There was a light easterly breeze and the sea was relatively calm with the normal long rolling North Atlantic swell, but the barometer was falling steadily. The *Trefusis* had a very small wheelhouse, just big enough for the helmsman, so officers kept their watch out on the open bridge. At about 1120 hours ship's time, I heard the faint but unmistakeable sound of an aeroplane from somewhere abaft the starboard beam. The sky was fully overcast with, I would estimate, the cloud base at about 2,000 feet, but there were some small breaks here and there. I picked up the binoculars and searched the cloud from where I heard the aeroplane sound coming. For a very brief moment, I saw a small seaplane passing through a break in the cloud, and then it was gone. I called the commodore ship, which was leading column 5, by Aldis lamp and reported that I had sighted a seaplane. The commodore asked me to confirm that it was a seaplane, which I did, and of course reported it to my own captain.

I have read many accounts of the *Jervis Bay* convoy, but none has ever mentioned a plane being sighted on the morning of 5 November, and I wonder if I was the only one to see it. My captain reported it to the RN officer when he was debriefed on our arrival in the UK, and I was later interviewed by an RN debriefing officer and told my story to him.

To return to 5 November, at noon our sights gave us a position of latitude 52° 29' N, longitude 33° 10' W, almost exactly halfway home. As is the time-honoured custom on board tramp ships, the third mate goes on the bridge at 2 bells, 1700 hours, to take the watch while the first mate gets his evening meal. This I did at 1700 on 5 November 1940. When I took over, the convoy was as normal, but the ship ahead of us, the *Briarwood*, was flying a flag signal which, when decoded, meant 'Attention is drawn to the bearing 330°.' I noticed that the commodore ship was flying the answering pendant, meaning that the signal was understood, so I took the bridge telescope and looked along the bearing 330°. There I saw a battleship almost hull-down. As I looked, I saw some flashes coming from it and at first thought it was signalling, but a few seconds later the first salvo of 11-inch shells came howling over and life became hectic.

The first salvo from the *Admiral Scheer*, as the battleship turned out to be, fell short but in line with the *Jervis Bay*, which up until then had been in its usual station within the convoy, between the fourth and fifth columns and abreast the of the second ships in those columns. The *Jervis Bay* now put on speed to draw clear of the convoy and the commodore ship signalled the convoy to alter course 40° to starboard, but before this alteration could be implemented, the second salvo of shells had landed close to the *Jervis Bay* and the commodore ordered the convoy to scatter. As the *Jervis Bay* pulled clear of the convoy and altered course towards the *Admiral Scheer*, the third salvo made a direct hit on her between her bridge and funnel, and I could see flames and smoke rising from her. Every salvo after that seemed to score a direct hit, and she was soon a blazing inferno.

Masters of ships in the convoy were given scattering procedures according to various textbook patterns, but due to the presence of the *Admiral Scheer* on the port side of the convoy, HX 84's scatter was by no means a textbook affair. With many ships, including the *Trefusis*, dropping smoke floats, along with the gathering dusk, some ships (not the *Trefusis*) firing their aft guns, and all ships having the same thought in mind to put their sterns to the *Admiral Scheer* and all speed on their engines, 'chaotic' would be a fair description of the scatter. The *Trefusis* had several near miss encounters with other ships of the convoy during the scatter, and to me it is remarkable that there were no collisions. The *Trefusis* was probably the slowest ship in the convoy, and a coal-burner, and many ships passed us at close quarters, some very close.

Having more or less disposed of the *Jervis Bay*, the *Admiral Scheer* now turned its attention to the merchant ships; one of them, the tanker *San Demetrio*, which had shortly before passed us at close quarters, was hit and caught fire, adding to the general mayhem. Darkness was by now almost total and the *Admiral Scheer* started using a searchlight to find its targets. So every time we saw the flashes of its guns or its searchlight, we put our stern to that position and steamed away as fast as our engines could take us. We saw several explosions when the *Admiral Scheer*'s guns scored a hit but, thankfully, we noticed that the action was taking place further and further from us. By 2200 hours, the gun flashes and the flames of ships on fire had all but dipped below the horizon. We found that we were heading northwards, and we decided to continue on that course for the rest of the night.

Next morning, we found that we were alone on a wide, wide sea. The wind had increased to gale force from the north-east and the poor old *Trefusis*, with her low power and deck cargo, was making heavy weather of it. The captain opened his emergency routing instructions and found that we were supposed to make a rendezvous position which was quite close to the coast of Northern Ireland. He decided that it would be better to continue northwards, away from the scene of the HX 84 battle. For the next four days, we only averaged 6.4 knots and, in fact, our day's run ending noon, 9 November was only 107 miles, giving 4.5 knots. Our noon position on the 9th was latitude 59.18 N, longitude 18.11 W. Because of our position, the weather conditions and reports of U-boat activity in the North Channel approaches, our captain decided to make the Clyde via the Minches, which was against Admiralty instructions not to proceed independently in the Minches. It was a decision that was to have tragic consequences.

Shortly before 2000 hours on 11 November, I went on the bridge to relieve the first mate. It was a wild night with a strong easterly wind and frequent rain showers, in between which the moon would briefly appear. The mate told me to be on the lookout for fishermen, as he had seen several, so as soon as he had left the bridge, which was about 2002 hours (he rarely gave what I would call a good handover of watch), I took up the binoculars and started scanning the horizon, starting on the port beam. When I got to about one point on the port bow I saw a dark shape, which at first I thought was land but then realised was a ship. I put my hand into the wheelhouse to put our navigation light master switch on but found that it was already in the 'ON' position, so I shouted 'Starboard' to the helmsman, and blew one short blast on the ship's whistle. The other ship then put its navigation lights on, from which I could see that it was crossing our bow finely from port to starboard. I then shouted 'Hard to starboard,' gave another short blast on the whistle and put the engine room telegraph to 'full astern'. To my consternation, the other ship then blew a two short blasts signal, signifying that it was turning to port, and at 2008 hours, the *Trefusis* struck the other ship at a nearly 90° angle between her bridge and her funnel (which was aft).

Our engines had not been going astern until after we hit, so the full momentum of the *Trefusis* went into the collision. After we had drawn away from the other ship, which proved to be the *Duchess*, a 1,200dwt coaster straggling behind a northbound convoy through which the *Trefusis* had unknowingly steamed (during the first mate's watch and which he thought were fishermen), she Morsed us: 'Sinking – send boat.' I asked our captain if I should take a boat away and he agreed.

I need to relate why I found it impossible to put on our navigation lights, the master switch being already in the 'ON' position. The *Trefusis* was one of those ships that, when our degaussing coils were energised, had insufficient electrical capacity to provide any other electrical facilities apart from emergency navigation lights. Because the captain wanted a light in his cabin to do the ship's accounts, he got an engineer to take a lead from the navigation light circuit. However, this meant that the master switch had to remain on and the individual navigation light switches off. The individual light switches were on the lower bridge, which entailed the officer of the watch leaving the bridge to put them on – an impossibility in a swift emergency, as this collision was.

Launching that heavy old wooden oar-propelled lifeboat in total darkness into a lumpy sea was difficult, to say the least. I got six volunteers to man the boat with me: four firemen, a steward and one AB. Our captain had taken the *Trefusis* up to windward of the *Duchess*, which was still afloat with its lights on, so that we could row downwind to her. However, as soon as we left the lee of the *Trefusis*, I heard cries of 'Help' coming from the water to windward of us. I tried to head towards the cries, but in the weather circumstances and sea state, we didn't have enough muscle power to pull the heavy boat to windward; the boat's head fell off the wind as each wave hit it. We tried our utmost but, tragically, the cries got weaker and weaker until we heard them no more.

The *Duchess* was still afloat to leeward and we saw some of her lights flashing on and off, so I concluded that someone was still on board and made for her. On manoeuvring alongside, we saw, as her stern rose in the seas, that her propeller was still turning, and getting the boat alongside her without being struck by it was quite tricky; she was only 190ft long and had a large wooden rubbing band just above the waterline. When alongside, one man jumped into the boat. When I yelled 'Tell the rest to hurry along!', he said he was the only one left on board. It appears that he was the cook/steward and had been in his bunk when the collision occurred. By the time he got on deck, he found that the other eleven men in the crew had (in spite of having asked the *Trefusis* to send a boat) launched their lifeboat, but it had overturned as soon as it left the ship's lee and all were thrown into the water. We returned to the *Trefusis*, from which we had been away for three hours.

We passed Ailsa Craig in the evening of 12 November (a week had already gone since the *Admiral Scheer* had attacked HX 84), and anchored in Rothesay Bay in the morning of the 13th, after suffering yet another collision when an outward-bound Swedish ship struck us amidships, fortunately in our bunker spaces. The *Trefusis* was one of the last surviving ships of HX 84 to reach the UK, the last being the *San Demetrio*, for which we all stood at the rail as she went past with SOS painted on her shell-damaged deckhouse – a sight I will never forget.

As to the attack on HX 84, the *Jervis Bay* seemed to be taken as much by surprise as the rest of us were, and as she was there to offer protection to the convoy, it is difficult to see what else she could have done but to turn towards the attacker. But knowing she was completely out-gunned, out-ranged and out-classed by the *Admiral Scheer*, it was incredibly brave to offer herself as a certain, but vain, sacrifice and uphold the honourable traditions of the Royal Navy. According to Captain Krancke, the commander of the *Admiral Scheer*, she drew his fire for 'exactly 22 minutes and 22 seconds'. This was valuable scattering time for the convoy, but my notes, written shortly after the event, concluded, 'darkness saved most ships'.

I sometimes wonder whether the *Admiral Scheer* would have attacked the convoy at all if Krancke knew that his spotter plane had been sighted, as from his own account he was as nervous as a kitten of meeting anything capable of firing back at him. The reason he gives for attacking the convoy so close to dusk was because, by next morning, the convoy would have been 100 miles nearer to the Western Approaches, where British naval units would be lurking, and would possibly be in range of shore-based aircraft.

Chapter Four

A Prisoner of War

Despite achieving only moderate results with the Q-ship in the 1914–18 conflict, the Royal Navy entered the Second World War determined to continue with the idea. The German Navy, on the other hand, had moved on, and was converting suitable merchant ships as commerce raiders. One of the first of these to set sail was the auxiliary cruiser *Pinguin*. Originally the *Kandelfels* of the Hansa Line, she was a 7,766-ton motor vessel requisitioned by the Kriegsmarine in late 1939 and fitted out for raiding. Her main armament consisted of six 150mm guns, one 75mm cannon, one twin 37mm and four 20mm anti-aircraft guns, and two torpedo tubes with sixteen torpedoes. She also carried two Heinkel spotter planes. She was under the command of Kapitän zur See Ernst-Felix Krüder, and carried a naval crew of 400.

Disguised as the Russian freighter *Petschura*, the *Pinguin* entered the North Atlantic via the Denmark Strait in June 1940, and captured or sank eleven Allied merchant ships as she moved south. Her twelfth victim was Port Line's *Port Brisbane*, which she stopped and sank on 20 November 1940.

The following was contributed by John D. Stevenson, AMI. Mar. E.:

My late father was second engineer on the *Port Brisbane* at the time of her sinking by the *Pinguin*.

He was, understandably, very reticent to discuss his experiences while a POW; however, I will relate a few points that I recall, and trust they may be of interest. I have two photographs of my father from this period; the first is of the crew of the *Port Brisbane* taken on board the raider and received by my late mother in the autumn of 1941.

The other is taken in the POW camp Marlag und Milag Nord, which, I understand, lay between Hamburg and Bremen. This was received during 1942. Unfortunately, there is no record of who the other personnel are, other than they are from the MN, although one is Tommy Reilly, a Canadian who became quite famous as a harmonica player in the Larry Adler mould, appearing on BBC Radio in productions such as *The Ted Ray Show* after the war. A second one was Archie Hart, who had been a well-known pro footballer with the Scottish club Third Lanark. They were both on the *Pinguin*, but from which ship, or ships, I do not know.

Father joined what was then the Commonwealth and Dominion Line in January 1921 as sixth engineer of the *Port Victor*, serving with both Port Line and Cunard until his retiral as chief engineer of the *Port Auckland* in 1961.

The *Port Brisbane* signed on at Liverpool on 1 August 1940. My mother decided to take my younger brother and me to Liverpool to visit my father (this was at the height of the Blitz, and we spent more time in the cellar under the digs in Cable Road, Bootle, as we did outside!), as his previous voyage on the same ship had ended in Liverpool on 14 July, no leave being granted.

As you know, the ship was sunk on 21 November 1940. Mother received a telegram to that effect from the War Office in late November, followed by a letter of confirmation from Port Line, with the same news, but also advising that my late father's wages would cease to be paid from the day of the sinking of the vessel.

Nothing further was heard other than that one lifeboat containing some twenty-five members of the crew, under the command of Mr Dingle, had been found by an RAN warship, but that my father was not among those rescued. In May 1941, my father was 'presumed dead, lost at sea' and my mother was awarded a widow's pension of around £3 per week, with 7s 10d for me and 3s 10d per week for my brother. Up to then we had been relying on savings and support from my father's family, who were Newhaven fisherfolk, and a very close-knit community.

In August of the same year, a postcard was received from my father, via the Red Cross, to the effect that he had been 'landed at Bordeaux, and was now a prisoner of war of the Third Reich'.

I was then 9, and vividly remember my mother being almost inconsolable. A few weeks later, when she received an OHMS letter to the effect that as she was no longer a widow, would she please refund the fourteen weeks' pension paid to her! Failure to do so carried the penalty of a fine, or possibly imprisonment.

Odd letters then began to filter through, from which we understood that Father had been taken to Stalag XB, which appeared to be a transit camp, and thence to Marlag und Milag Nord, where the prisoners were expected to work on the local farms.

As I stated earlier, Father did not discuss to any great length his experiences relating to the sinking and his time on the raider, but for what it is worth, I will recount what I remember.

The vessel had left Australia with instructions to run at maximum speed alone for Cape Town, where bunkers were available (she was a coal-burner). There was no intelligence regarding enemy vessels in the area.

In the early hours of the morning in question, a shell was fired across the ship, and Father, who was off duty and asleep, was awakened by the general alarm. He picked up his gold hunter watch, his false teeth, and a small bag of personal belongings and went below. The master, Captain Steel, called for full revs, but a second shell hit the wireless room, killing the operator.

Details regarding the abandonment of the ship are rather sketchy, but it appears that Mr Dingle's boat slid away astern under the cover of darkness, and escaped.

Father sustained a severe hernia on leaving the vessel and had nothing but praise for the medical attention he received on the *Pinguin*. However, their quarters were in the upper tween decks, with greatly restricted ventilation, especially in stormy weather, and this, coupled with the fact that the mattresses were bags of salt, caused problems generally, but especially where prisoners had cuts or broken skin. He reckoned he lost 2 stone in weight during the six months on the raider.

Boredom was obviously the greatest problem, and some older men found it extremely difficult to cope, although it seems that being typically British, 'necessity became the mother of invention'; packs of playing cards were made, draughtsmen were carved.

I understand that there were two instances where the prisoners were battened down due to the close proximity of Allied vessels or planes.

Father held a great dislike for Germans in general. This was born out of the fact that they had taken away his freedom for five years of his life, and I can understand that, but at the same time he always spoke well of the crew of the raider – I suppose they were seamen, no matter which side they were on.

Jim Waggot, who was serving as a quartermaster in the *Port Wellington*, sister ship to the *Port Brisbane*, when she was sunk by the *Pinguin*, went into greater detail when I contacted him.

The food on the raider was edible but not as plentiful as one would wish; already we were thinking about the food we had wasted on the *Port Wellington*. We remained on board the raider for two weeks, during which time she appeared to be engaged in minelaying. The prison space we were occupying had rails running through it, and every so often a mine would be wheeled through on its way aft. Later we learned that the Germans had mined the harbour entrance at Sydney.

Several days later, the raider appeared to be steaming south, for it was getting much colder, and on 15 December 1940, we were transferred to the Norwegian oil tanker *Storstad*, which the Germans had captured. The transfer was carried out by motor launch and the sea was like a millpond. Our destination, we were informed, was Nazi Germany; however, we wouldn't get there, would we? What about the British Royal Navy – they ruled the waves, didn't they?

The *Storstad* had been captured intact and carried a full cargo of fuel oil, and was to be used during our time on board to refuel U-boats and pocket battleships. Already the German engineers from the *Pinguin* had laid rails at the after end to facilitate the laying of sea mines in major sea lanes around the Australian coastline. She was worked by the Norwegian crew, who were threatened with reprisals against their families were they not to co-operate. The German prize crew consisted of no more than twenty men under the command of Leutnant Helmut Hanfield, who had been a watch officer on the *Pinguin*.

The ratings, 300 of us, were placed in the forward general cargo hold, which was accessed by a small booby hatch. Daily exercise was permitted, twelve prisoners being allowed out of the hold at one time for ten minutes. We estimated that to clear the hold in an emergency would take thirty minutes. However, the cover of the booby hatch was closed and locked at nightfall, and there was no guarantee that in an emergency, the Germans would unlock it.

Christmas Day 1940, as a treat we were offered an extra ten minutes' exercise. The weather was cold and as we were scantily clad we declined the offer, which annoyed the Germans. At

2.00 p.m., Old Charlie Kronberg, a Latvian aged 62, passed away. He was a greaser off the *Port Wellington* and had been a crew member for sixteen years. Although we were to be starved, cold, short of clothing and suffer from extreme heat, Charlie was our only loss during this terrible voyage.

It would be difficult for the reader to visualise how twenty Germans could control prisoners made up as follows: 300 ratings, some fifty officers and captains, and ten passengers. However, the various sections of prisoners were segregated from each other, the prison spaces were fitted with explosive charges controlled from the bridge, and the watchkeeper guards were armed with machine guns and hand grenades. Many plans were discussed for overthrowing the Germans and taking the ship, but when examined thoroughly they were not considered feasible. In the lower hold, we discovered the ship's mooring ropes and cut them up by chafing them against the steel joists. We then teased them out and made some sort of mattresses to lay on the steel deck plates. The toilet facilities were 40-gallon oil drums with the tops cut off and one squatted on top, keeping up a conversation with all and sundry. Each morning, the toilets were emptied, it being a difficult task to pull them up through the booby hatch without spilling.

Our voyage on the *Storstad* was for a duration of seven weeks, during which the climate changed continually; we went from extreme cold to extreme heat, from calm weather to rough weather. The washing facilities consisted of a salt-water hosepipe on deck during the ten-minute exercise period.

Whenever the *Storstad* made a rendezvous with a German warship or submarine, we were brought onto the deck to observe the might of the German Navy. The rendezvous were made near to the equator. At one such meeting, the German Navy was towing a captured British merchant ship, the *Duquesa*, a fridge ship bound from the Argentine with meat and eggs. On that day we were given several boiled eggs each. The outcome can be imagined.

Gradually, the weather again became colder and the sea rougher, and we estimated that we were approaching the Bay of Biscay. On 4 February 1941, the miserable voyage ended. Nothing in the future could be worse than that – or could it?

Our destination turned out to be Bordeaux, where we were gathered on the quayside, counted, recounted, and then marched off for many miles to Frontstalag 221, located at the village of Saint-Médard-en-Jalles. At this camp, the food was of poor quality and in short supply, but we did have fresh air and plenty of drinking water, which was much appreciated after the voyage on the *Storstad*.

On Monday, 12 March 1941, the German officer in charge of Frontstalag 221 informed us that on the next day we would be transported by passenger train to a nice camp in Germany, with good food and sporting facilities. The journey would take three days. The transport was via cattle wagons only just vacated by horses. The food ration soon ran out, and the journey took six days. So, we waved farewell to France.

The journey ended at midnight on 18 March after having travelled through Liège, Aachen, Cologne, Düsseldorf, Hamm, Münster, Oldenburg, Rotenburg and Bremervörde, the distance having been extended owing to the attentions of the Royal Air Force. Then we were dragged out of the train and marched off many miles to the 'wonderful' camp we had been looking forward to.

We were soon to learn that Sandbostel was to be crueller than anything else we had suffered to date. Arriving in the dead of night, we were searched by over-enthusiastic French prisoners; we were fingerprinted and allocated a number, mine being 87919, and given a numbered medallion to be worn around the neck. At daylight, we were marched through the main camp, passing hordes of prisoners of every possible nationality – French, Russians, Serbs, Poles and German political internees. The clothing was also strange: French uniforms, civilian clothes and the striped pyjama type of prison uniform favoured by the German authorities in jails and concentration camps. Our tour ended at the compounds reserved for the British merchant seamen. Others had preceded us and put some sort of order into camp life. The barracks were either divided into twelve rooms, accommodating eighteen prisoners in each room of three-tier bunks, or large open-plan halls with three-tier shelving jutting out into the centre. This type held 300 prisoners.

Conditions could not have been worse. The ground was a quagmire, and the Dutch wooden clogs we were now wearing stuck in the mud and left our feet as we walked. Food was regular: a bucket of fish head soup once per day for twenty-four prisoners. The prisoners collected the soup from the main kitchen, which was staffed by French internees. The French prisoners received the thicker soup from the bottom of the soup boiler but all other nationals received the thinner soup from the top. On one occasion, a Russian prisoner jumped the counter and tipped the French cook into his boiler of soup. The others and I did not remain around to witness the outcome.

We were to stay at Sandbostel for fourteen months. The deprivation was unbelievable. Food shortages, strenuous working parties and illness all took their toll on our numbers.

I was engaged on a working party cutting and stacking peat, working in freezing water up to the knees, wheeling the cut peat to the stacking area in ancient wheelbarrows that had minds of their own. When I think of Sandbostel, I can still feel the cold winds blowing over the North German moor. A typhus epidemic broke out amongst the prisoners in the main compound, and the number of deaths was unbelievable. Each night, death carts would be wheeled out of the camp full of corpses. The epidemic was aggravated and prolonged by the prisoners hiding their dead comrades under the floorboards of the barracks in order to collect their rations. At that time, we in the Merchant Navy compound had received inoculations, which, combined with the isolation from the others, staved off the epidemic.

During this period, the International Red Cross committee paid its first visit to the camp and intervened on our behalf, suggesting that the Geneva Convention was not being adhered to. It paid off, and within six months, we were rehoused at Milag Nord Camp in the village of Westertimke.

In the September of 1942, I left Sandbostel. It was a red-letter day for me; we walked the 12 miles to Milag with joy in our hearts. It was like a liberation. We stayed overnight in a village hall before proceeding on to Milag, where we were reunited with our friends who had gone on before.

Sandbostel was liberated by the Guards Armoured Division on 30 April 1945, and the conditions met with by the soldiers were as bad as any of the concentration camps later discovered. Conditions had deteriorated greatly since I had left there, although at the time of my internment I would not have believed it was possible.

John Stevenson concludes the story:

My father returned from Germany, complete with demob suit, on 24 May 1945, and signed on 16 July 1945 in Glasgow as chief engineer of the *Fort Chambly* for a voyage to India. A total leave of forty-seven days after five years!

Incidentally, he was eventually paid 50 per cent of the salary he would have earned in the five years he was a POW. The covering letter, if it could be called that, stated: 'This is a goodwill payment' on behalf of the shipowners and not the

Government, who were completely disinterested. My parents had taken their case to the local Labour MP, but eventually gave up and accepted the 50 per cent offered.

From this point, my father became extremely bitter with regard to the treatment of MN personnel during and immediately after the war compared with that given to returning 'combatants', but that is another story.

My brother and I both went to sea with Port Line as engineers before following our careers with other employers.

Chapter Five

A Voyage to Remember

Convoy SLS 64, which sailed from Freetown on 30 January 1941, consisted of nineteen ships: twelve British, four Greek and three Norwegian. They were all elderly tramps that would be hard-pressed to maintain 7 or 8 knots in a fair wind, and all deep laden with cargoes desperately needed in the United Kingdom. This was a convoy worthy of maximum protection, yet it sailed alone.

Eyewitnesses testified that when the convoy left Freetown, there were fourteen Royal Navy ships anchored in the harbour – four light cruisers, a sloop, four corvettes and five armed trawlers – all apparently uncommitted. Yet the convoy was allowed to sail unescorted into U-boat-infested waters, with the added danger of a beast like the 32-knot, 8-inch gun cruiser *Admiral Hipper* on the prowl. The end result was eight ships and their precious cargoes sent to the bottom, along with the irredeemable loss of 153 lives. To coin a phrase: 'The mind boggles.'

The *Margot* was one of the lucky ones, escaping the guns of the *Admiral Hipper* by the quick thinking of Captain Price, who resorted to a subterfuge that was then widely used by British merchantmen when attacked by a surface raider. He avoided the attention of the German gunners by burning smoke floats on board to give the appearance of a ship on fire, and then took to the boats with the intention of reboarding as soon as the raider, satisfied that the ship was abandoned and sinking, had gone away. The chair-bound directors of Kaye Bros., in their complete ignorance of how the war at sea was being fought, accused Price of leaving his ship open to a salvage claim, and sacked him. Once again, there are no words to describe this stupid action.

The *Margot*'s long seagoing career ended some sixteen months after the *Admiral Hipper* incident, when she was torpedoed and sunk off the east coast of the United States by *U-588* while carrying a cargo of military stores to Alexandria. Captain Ifor Llewellyn Price had moved on by then, to be replaced by Captain Henry Bell Collins. Only one man was lost, and the sinking ended amicably, with Collins and the U-boat's commander, Korvettenkapitän Viktor Vogel, who was an ex-merchant seaman, swopping reminiscences of mutual friends in the River Plate over a bottle of rum. The two captains even arranged to meet again after the war, and no doubt would have done so, had they lived. Viktor Vogel was lost with *U-588* and all his crew just two months later, while Henry Collins went down with his next command, the *Empire Turnstone*, in October 1942. It was a cruel war for both sides.

John Cave, first radio officer of the *Margot*, gives his version of events:

The return voyage [the *Margot* was homeward-bound from Suez after delivering supplies to the 8th Army] was uneventful until we were in the Mozambique Channel on Christmas Day 1940. Suddenly, the engine room telegraph rang out on the bridge, and the engines came to a sudden halt. Everybody was shocked. We were now a sitting target. Things had been going well for a while, and I'd even written a verse for the ship's menu:

> The *Margot* was sailing in tropical seas
> As the time of the feasting grew near
> The Mates were thinking of duck and green peas
> While the Engineers' thoughts turned to beer.

The Cook looked worried on the twenty-fourth
And the Stewards appeared that way too,
For they thought of the abuse the men would use
When they knew it was Irish stew.

There was an unnatural silence while the engineers worked to get the engine going again. Without being told, everyone began to appreciate the hard way how very easily sound travelled in a metal structure. Every saucepan in the galley, the movement of a shovel in the stokehold, or a spanner dropping on engine room plates seemed to create such a terrific noise that, in our minds, all the submarines in the area must have heard it and would now be heading our way.

Suddenly, the eerie silence was broken by the engine room telegraph ringing on the bridge. The engines were now ready. The message was answered, the ship came to life, and the pleasant sound of crankshaft thumping was heard once again. We had been drifting in a 3 or 4-knot current for the last two or three days and by now were almost clear of Madagascar island.

After calling for bunkers in South Africa, we continued a normal voyage to Freetown, Sierra Leone, for convoy to the UK. Leaving Freetown and heading north, Gibraltar was past our beam and we stood well clear of Cape St Vincent at 37° 12' N, 21° 20' W, where we expected to rendezvous with another convoy on that fateful morning, 12 February 1941. The radio officer got involved in a lot of visual signalling in those days, and I had already 'bent on' AM, a flag signal of welcome, and taken it to the top of the halyards, to be 'broken' when the other convoy, or its escorts searching for us, was sighted.

Our convoy position was 11, which meant that we were leading ship in the port column, and probably amongst the first to spot the arrivals. On the bridge, binoculars were trained on the direction from where the convoy was expected to appear. Promptly, at the expected time of seven o'clock, the mate shouted that he could make out one of the escorts. It was fortunate for us that the commodore (in *Warlaby*, position 31, if I remember correctly) carried a naval signalling crew, and beat us to it, for I can still see the forward guns of that 'escort' turning towards the convoy, as the commodore had been identified. Of that moment, I cannot describe my feelings. It was not fear or terror, but the apprehension that we were going to be shot at. I had read about such things, even thought about them, and wondered what would happen and what I would do if it did happen to me. Now, my turn had really come.

The next few minutes became total bedlam, as if the raising of a flag had started some sort of hell. What a little while before had been taken to be our escort had now turned into a terrible monster. Shells passed over us to find their targets on the rearmost, defenceless ships. Some were blowing their whistles to attract attention, while others were on fire. At least three had been hit and were either on fire, or sinking. But no help was forthcoming.

At the time, the attacker could only be identified as a pocket battleship, but later it was confirmed that she had been the heavy cruiser named after Admiral Franz von Hipper. She had eight 8-inch guns, and a speed of 32 knots to get herself out of trouble, though from commissioning she had suffered engine defects, and relied on short 'commerce raiding' skirmishes.

Without realising, I found myself in the radio room reading a scrap of paper on which was our last four-hourly position. If we had been sailing independently, the first thing would have been to transmit a special raider message on the distress frequency and include this position. As it was, this was left to the commodore, but he had been one of the first to go, identified from his flag hoists. I put on the headphones and listened. Several ships were using their radios and it was very conflicting. Suddenly, an idea flashed through my mind.

I started up the old spark transmitter, and using our international call sign sent a raider (RRRR) distress message, giving our position and a description of the attack. Pausing to listen for any acknowledgement, which did not come, I used the collective naval call sign (GBZZ), usually reserved for those seeking assistance when attacked by pirates in the China seas, and 'answered' a mythical warship, using operators' slang abbreviations and finishing with, of all things, 'Good morning, see you soon.' What the operator on the *Admiral Hipper* said, did or thought is questionable, but from then on the situation changed for the better, and the shelling seemed to stop.

I knew that our 4.7-inch gun had been firing while I was sending the fictitious message, and getting no answer from the bridge voice pipe, I went up to tell the Old Man what I'd done and that the code and other confidential books had been dumped. Everything seemed to be at a standstill. All around us was smoke, and then I noticed that the crew were already in two lifeboats and were apparently standing by for the Old Man and me. I found him in the chartroom ramming the local chart down his life jacket. 'Go down to my room, Sparks,' he said, 'and get out two glasses.' He followed me down the ladder and by the time I'd put the glasses on a table, he was already pouring out two full tumblers of whisky. I didn't even feel it go down, but well remember the pair of us hanging on to the rope ladder until the opportunity came to jump on a thwart as the boat came alongside, bucking madly in the high swell.

Every now and then, we would hear loud thumps, and we all joined in sympathy for the lads of those ships that were being slowly and methodically finished off by the *Hipper*. It was some time before anybody realised that the large watertight biscuit container slung under one of the thwarts was the culprit as it responded in drumlike thuds to the motion of the boat.

After a while, hearing no other noises, the captain told everybody to keep a sharp lookout for that second or two while the boat was at the crest of the wave. As we came up, the *Margot* was still plainly in sight, and before we went down into the trough of the wave, another lifeboat was spotted. The Old Man stood up and had a good look at it the next time as we rose on the swell. 'She's from the *Volturno*,' he shouted, and then to those on the oars, 'Row, you buggers! If he gets there first he'll claim salvage.' We went down into the trough, and without further ado he brought the helm hard over and we were headed back to our ship. But he needn't have worried so much. The other boat was headed for his own ship, too.

Making fast to the rope ladder that we had so recently left, everybody clambered back on board as if it had been a boat drill. The engineers went to raise steam, the catering staff to raise some sort of a meal, and then the boats had to be got back on board. The bosun, a small bald-headed Cockney from East London, stayed aboard to hook on the blocks and was coming up with the first boat when a twist in the rope fouled a sheave. Attacking the problem with his marlin spike, the rope suddenly cleared, but the jerk of the heavy boat was too much for an old davit, which started to buckle. Everybody shouted, but there was little the bosun could do about it except grab for a rope, which he missed, and went hurtling into the sea, some 40 feet below. By now, the second boat had come alongside and did a superbly exaggerated rescue job among fictional shark fins that apparently kept 'appearing'. (Reliving these scenes of laughter and enjoyment when, a short while previously, those sailors were facing enemy gunfire and death, worries me about the reports of today's 'manhood'.)

As far as we were able to find out at the time, at least five British ships (*Warlaby, Westbury, Shrewsbury, Oswestry Grange* and *Derrynane*) were lost, although there were others of foreign register. The action lasted approximately twenty minutes, if my memory serves me right, but apart from a mention in Churchill's History, Volume 3, page 104, and *The Atlantic Star 1939–45* by David A. Thomas, where, on page 59, there is another eyewitness account, I have unfolded little except to have correspondence with the captain of the *Neritina* (Shell), who was the son of the captain of the *Blairatholl*, and Bruce Scott, who was the son of the chief engineer of the *Derrynane*.

Soon, the four British ships (*Margot, Volturno, Clunepark* and *Blairatholl*) and two Greeks, I believe, were able to get underway again. As vice commodore, we were now responsible for assembling the others, and soon we had all set off, line astern, for the nearest friendly port, Funchal, Madeira.

Once there at a safe anchorage, the consul wanted to see both the Old Man and myself. During the interrogation I was confronted with a long, typewritten document which astonished me as I began to read. It was word for word the message that I had transmitted before the shelling ended and the raider disappeared. Seeing this, it was hard to believe that I'd sent so much stuff in what appeared to be such a short time. It included the false receipt I'd given to the fictitious warship, and I was thoroughly questioned about that, as well as the twiddlybits of unofficial operating procedure I'd used. Afterwards, the consul entertained the two of us in Theo's, a few doors away from the consulate.

The next day, the captain and the mate went ashore to the agents. They must have been enjoying themselves, for that evening, a hurricane warning was received and we anxiously awaited their return. In the meantime, the weather got up so quickly that no boat would take them off, and we could not remain where we were in case any one of us dragged an anchor. So, the second mate, who thankfully was an experienced seaman, decided to put to sea and ride out the storm.

The third mate went forward and started to raise the anchor, but when it was just below the hawsepipe, and the ship was way on, the gypsy ring broke, and the windlass became useless. The chain being temporarily held on the brake, it was decided that the anchor should be lowered and the cable let go in the chain locker. Soon, the effect of the long pendulum made the ship 'stiff' and unable to respond to the storm, which by now was battering her boat deck and everything on it.

To save both the ship and those on board, the cable would have to be cut. But no such cutting or burning gear was on board, the only tool being a hacksaw. I shall never forget the few days of that terrifying storm. At the time, not one of us would admit to any fear, but the violent, unusual motions of the ship at the mercy of the huge waves and the fearful strain the bow was taking as it tried to break away from the restraining chain and respond to the sea, together with the constant screaming of wind through the rigging, were terrible. Each one of us must have had our own thoughts on how much longer the 'spec job' hull could sustain such a battering. The thought of the ship foundering at any moment brought out a herd instinct and many of us slept together on the saloon deck, although no one would admit to suggesting it.

Working in relays under appalling conditions in the chain locker, the engineers took almost two days to cut through a cable link. The vessel responded immediately. Her head came round into the wind, and the incessant heavy pitching, rolling and pounding ceased, to a great extent. Three days later, the storm had blown itself out and we were steaming back to Funchal. The other ships had already arrived, and greeted us with a chorus of their whistles. Apparently, they had given us up for lost. We couldn't join them at anchor, of course, and spent several hours steaming up and down until a berth was cleared for us at the one and only jetty. We had not been tied up for very long before the damage inspection took place. It was far worse than anticipated.

A few days later, a meeting was arranged with all crew present. We had to decide on one of two things. It was obvious that the *Margot* had suffered severe damage, and it would be many weeks before she could be made completely seaworthy. Did we feel we should stay that long? Alternatively, if we were to proceed immediately, a strong escort to Britain would be assured.

The decision was not an easy one. The local Portuguese inhabitants and the evacuees from Gibraltar were going out of their way to give us all a good time. Few barmen would charge us for cigarettes, and there always seemed to be someone at your elbow to offer a drink. Understandably, not one of us was inclined to leave this paradise for a while and we began to appreciate the agonies Fletcher Christian must have suffered. However, patriotism prevailed, and within a few days, we had all volunteered to go home with a strong escort, but without lifeboats or lifesaving equipment lost during the hurricane.

The locals got to hear about this and their admiration grew. Funchal was not a large place, and one final scene on the morning of departure will always remain in my mind. The jetty where we were tied up was really an extended breakwater on the northern side of town. As sailing time approached, a group of men in brilliant uniforms and carrying musical instruments arrived and took up their places at the end of the breakwater. By now, the breakwater was swarming with people, all looking anxiously at the sight of us, and then to seaward, where three destroyers were waiting for us at the 3-mile limit.

The ship had been dressed overall, which added to the gaiety of the occasion. As the ropes were let go, the band began to play, and for no good reason except for sheer excitement, the Old Man blew several long blasts on the whistle. The crowds became ecstatic, and it must have done quite a bit for public relations as the destroyers blew their sirens in response. The band continued until we could hardly hear their music, and then they stood up and waved their caps. The party was over, and with the other ships, we steamed towards our escort. However, we were bitterly disappointed to find that our escort had disappeared, and so we carried on together.

Our destination was Greenock, and it was there, on a particularly cold, dark night in March 1941, that the final episode in an eventful voyage took place.

The dockside, of course, was unlit and it was as black as pitch as I made my way ashore to post some letters. Suddenly and without any warning, I felt myself step into space, and a few moments later, I hit the water. I started to shout and after what seemed like an age, I heard voices, and then the beam of a torch started to search around the water until it found me, and then went out. By this time, my clothes were starting to get soaked, and I could feel myself getting lower in the stinking, oily water. I managed to struggle and swim about until there was a loud splash close by, and the torch shone again. This time it lit up the lifebuoy that had been thrown down, and I ducked under and thrust my arms through the cork ring. At least I felt a little safer now. Two men shouted that they would be back shortly, and again the light went out, leaving me in total darkness. Very soon, another lifebuoy landed alongside me, but this one had a rope attached.

Slowly I managed to get myself into the new buoy, as the freezing water was making any movement heavy going, and I was thankful when the men shouted to hold tight as they were going to pull me out. It was no easy job as by now my clothes had become thoroughly soaked. To try to help them I began to walk up the side of the dock, but this was hopeless, and after a while, they just dragged me, a pure deadweight, up the sides. The barnacles ruined my uniform, but I was beyond caring.

The men turned out to be dock police and they helped me to their hut at the dock gate. While waiting for the ambulance, they told me I had fallen into the James Watt dry dock, and that I was a very lucky person to fall into a dry dock while it was being filled. It was also another piece of luck that they had been passing so close at the time, otherwise nobody would have heard me shouting and my number would have been up. They told me they had got several out of that dock so far that year, but I'd been the first live one. It must have been 1 April, because I was in Greenock Infirmary for two days, and then signed off on 3 April.

There is a sequel to all this. Actually, there are two sequels. A couple of years ago I wrote a letter to *Sea Breezes* magazine asking if anybody else could recall the episode with the *Admiral Hipper*, and mentioned the ships concerned. By return of post, I had a very interesting reply from one Mr D.G. Stanley, which I quote verbatim:

> I particularly recall the *Margot*, my first ship when I went to sea as an apprentice in 1935. I remember my first meal aboard when I joined the ship at Liverpool – two large pork chops for tea – this could not be so bad, but little did I know that there was no refrigerator on board, only an ice box, and after the fresh stores were consumed we seemed to exist on dry salt fish and tinned rabbit, with an egg for breakfast on Sundays, while supplies lasted. It was a luxury when I was transferred to the *Marton*, another of the company's ships, with a fridge and two eggs a week, on Thursdays and Sundays.
>
> Sorry about this reminiscence... Following an accident on board I was working in Kaye's office in London (Kaye, Son

and Co Ltd, the owners) when the *Margot* returned to the UK after the encounter with the *Admiral Hipper*. Captain Price was summoned to the office to account for his actions. As I recall, his initial report was that when the convoy encountered the German raider, he set off all the smoke canisters on board, and with the entire crew abandoned ship. He claimed that by this action the enemy would assume the ship had been hit and was finished, and would cease their attack. This ruse was apparently successful. After the raider had disappeared, Captain Price and his crew returned to the ship and resumed the voyage. This action was not, however, approved by Sydney Kaye and his fellow directors. They took the view that by abandoning his ship, he had laid open the possibility of others boarding the vessel, which could have been lost in a heavy salvage claim, and by this thoughtless action Captain Price was dismissed from the company, despite intervention by Captain Coombs of the MNAOA.

John Cave continues:

A sequel to this sorry incident is an entry in the *London Gazette* dated 11 June 1941:

AWARD OF THE GEORGE MEDAL

Captain Ivor Llewellyn Price. The ship was attacked by a surface raider, the Master turned away and burnt smoke floats. Owing to the strong wind, these did not wholly screen the ship but gave better cover to three other ships, which escaped. Captain Price fired on the enemy when his guns bore and the raider directed his full attention to the ship, firing as he closed. The raider subsequently made off. Captain Price gathered together the ships remaining and after searching for and picking up survivors, proceeded to port.

Well, that is the official account of what happened. I, after all these years, would be interested to learn what actually took place. Did you all abandon ship, which seems to be the reason poor Captain Price got the sack?

The award must have been an embarrassment for the directors, as when Captain Price was in London on 23 October 1941 to receive the George Medal from King George VI at Buckingham Palace, he was not welcome at the office, and I, as a mere junior, was detailed to take him to lunch. This was the last I saw or heard of Captain Price, G.M.

Captain Price retained his position in the British Merchant Navy Officers' Pool, and was soon in command again. After the war, he seems to have dropped out of circulation, and I only recently received news of his whereabouts from his daughter, who accompanied him to Buckingham Palace. Apparently, his eyesight had started to fail, which made him unemployable for command, and he went out east, where the regulations were more lax. He eventually finished up as a master on the Hong Kong–Macau ferry service, where, in 1952, he was lost in a typhoon.

Chapter Six

The Last Voyage of the *Auditor*

The *Auditor*, owned by T & J Harrison of Liverpool, was a veteran of the Cape–India run, carrying manufactured goods outward to South and East African ports and produce homeward from India. Built on the Clyde in 1924, she was a coal-burning steamer powered by a three-cylinder, triple-expansion engine, giving her a speed of 12½ knots. In command was Captain Edwin Bennett, and she carried a total complement of seventy-six, of which fifty were lascar crewmen. On this, her final voyage, the *Auditor* was carrying a general cargo of 5,300 tons, with ten aircraft on her hatch tops.

This is an extract from the diary of the *Auditor*'s Second Radio Officer George V. Monk:

On 14 June 1941, I joined the SS *Auditor* (T & J Harrison), 5,444 grt. We sailed from the Royal Albert Docks, London, on 15 June for Cape Town, Durban and Beira, fully loaded with export cargo, army stores and aircraft.

At Southend-on-Sea we joined a northbound convoy, first calling at Methil before passing round the north of Scotland to Oban. When the convoy had just passed Flamborough Head, the ship ahead – a motor ship of Ellerman Lines – set off an acoustic mine, which exploded just under our bows. Fortunately, the mine had been laid in deep water and although it gave us a severe hammering, it did not damage the hull or engines. At that time, the merchant ships in east coast convoys were provided with an anti-aircraft balloon. One was delivered to us at Southend, which we would keep until Methil. It was flown just above the top of the foremast and let out several hundred feet when an aircraft attack was imminent. The balloon wire was wound onto a large drum attached to a cargo winch, but when the mine exploded, the shaking was so severe it loosened the controls and allowed the balloon to rise. It was some time before we realised what had occurred, and that our balloon was at the end of its tether. The commodore made some comments about playing with our balloon, not realising what had caused the problem.

The coastal convoy arrived at Oban on 20 June and the ocean convoy of some forty-five ships – OB 337 – sailed the next day. A week later, it dispersed and the merchantmen then sailed independently, bound for their first ports.

Naval Control at Oban had given our master a route that was to take the *Auditor* due south to the Brazilian coast and then across the South Atlantic to Cape Town. This route was planned to take us away from the area of U-boat activity, but it was never completed.

On 4 July 1941, just as the moon was setting at about 2.00 a.m., the *Auditor* was torpedoed by U-boat 123 (Lt Hardegen). A violent explosion took place in way of No. 4 hold port side, and it destroyed No. 4 lifeboat. I was asleep at the time the torpedo hit but quickly put on some clothes and grabbed my hammer bag and life jacket. Making my way to the radio office, which was on the boat deck aft of the funnel, I found that my chief was already there and had started transmitting our distress message:

SSSS SSSS SSSS AUDITOR 25.47N 28.23W
TORPEDOED

The emergency spark transmitter was being used, as the ship's power supply had failed. The chief knew the position at the time because at the start of each watch the radio office was given a half-hourly position report, which ensured no delay in getting the position.

The radio office had emergency lighting and I could see that it was in a shambles. Fortunately, the emergency transmitter was in working order and the aerial was intact. My chief called out to me: 'Get the lifeboat transmitter into No. 1 boat and I'll carry on here.' I left and made my way to No. 1 boat station under the bridge.

While at sea, lifeboats were always kept swung out and lowered to deck level so that, if required, they could be lowered without delay. However, just as I had lifted the portable transmitter into the lifeboat, the crew at the falls lowered away. When it was launched, the boat's rope ladder came down. As my station was in the chief officer's boat – No. 2 port side – I was now in the wrong boat, so I had to climb up the rope ladder to get back to the boat deck. While I was doing this I passed the third officer, who was descending. When I got back to the boat deck I saw Captain Bennett dressed in his shore clothes (he was concerned about being taken prisoner by the U-boat), and he called out: 'Go and get your chief – she's going fast.'

By this time, about seven minutes after the explosion, my eyes had become accustomed to the darkness and, as it was a clear night with stars shining brightly, I was able to move around the ship easily. When I got back to the radio office, I found that my chief was still transmitting our distress message. He asked me to get his coat from his room, which was on the lower deck.

This I did, and when I got there I could hear the sea pouring into the engine room below, just like the sound of a large waterfall. On returning to the radio office we checked that the codebooks had been thrown overboard, and my chief then screwed down the Morse key (so that any ship could get a bearing on us). We then quickly made our way back to the bridge deck.

The only lifeboat alongside was No. 1 – the captain's boat. I went down the rope ladder (the one I had recently climbed), followed by my chief and the captain. The boat rope was cut and we pulled away. When about 80 yards off and fifteen minutes after the torpedo hit, the *Auditor*'s bow slowly rose up until vertical, then she sank gracefully into the Cape Verde Basin, some 3,000 fathoms below. What was so ghastly to us was the noise of the ship breaking up: the engines, boilers and cargo breaking loose, and the flashes as wire ropes supporting the masts and deck cargo snapped and whipped around hitting other objects, also the anchor chains coming adrift. Besides wreckage floating around, all that was left of a fine ship were a number of large crates (deck cargo) and three boats.

A little later, the sound of diesels could be heard; it was *U-123* cruising around. Obviously, Lt Hardegen wanted to make sure that the *Auditor* had sunk, but he did not contact us.

There were twenty-three survivors in the captain's boat, which included the chief engineer, chief steward, third officer, chief radio officer (my chief), me, one AB, one gunner and fifteen lascars. Nothing could be done until daylight except to keep in touch with the other two boats. As our boat was leaking, it was necessary to bail continuously.

At sunrise on Friday, stocks were taken of our provisions and these were found to be one and a half kegs of water (about 9 gallons), one case of small tins of condensed milk and a large quantity of hard ship's biscuits.

The daily ration was:

half-dipper of water (3 fluid ounces)
one spoonful of condensed milk (spoon made from the wood
   of the case)
one biscuit (biscuits were so hard that they could not be eaten).

Later, the three boats closed up and the captain had a conference with the chief officer and second officer, who were in charge of boats No. 2 and No. 3 respectively. My chief told them that our distress signal had been acknowledged. Subsequently, it transpired that several ships had received it, and one with HF transmission had passed it direct to London. The naval authorities knew that we had been in action and the ship had sunk. The question was, would we be rescued or would we have to sail to the nearest land?

The conference was held while the boats were riding to sea anchors, which had been put out at daybreak. As we were in the zone of the north-easterly trade winds there was a stiff breeze blowing with a choppy sea, and it was difficult for the boats to keep together. So we secured a rope to each boat to stop us drifting apart.

Whilst the position given in our distress message was accurate, a decision had now to be taken as to the islands or land we should make for if we were not rescued. It was necessary to bear in mind the prevailing winds and ocean currents, and that we would be sailing a lifeboat without a keel and liable to drifting. Unfortunately, there were no Atlantic charts available, and the only navigational aid in each boat was a compass.

For many years before the war, I used to buy a pocket shipping diary, and when in London in 1940, I had purchased one for 1941. Little did I know then how useful it was going to be, because when the officers were conversing I suddenly realised that I had the diary in my coat. Many times in the past I had seen a couple of pages giving latitude and longitude of bunkering ports, and when I looked at this page it gave the co-ordinates for St Vincent – the port of the Cape Verde islands. As I also had my paybook in my hammer bag, I was able to draw a chart and lay off a course to St Vincent, which was some 600 miles SSE of our present position. With this information, it was decided that should we not be rescued, these islands were the obvious choice for a landfall. And so, the officers worked out a course for each to steer that would allow for the effects of the north-easterly trade winds, ocean current and drift. The estimated time for the voyage was eleven to twelve days. However, a factor that greatly influenced this decision was that the islands were mountainous. In fact, Captain Bennett had visited St Vincent many years before and remembered that these mountains were very high, around 6,000 to 9,000 feet, and therefore could be seen from a great distance, perhaps 40 miles or more. If they had been low-lying, the decision would have been, no doubt, to set course for the north-east coast of South America – some 1,700 miles distant, and a voyage of around twenty-one days or more.

At the Ocean Convoy Conference in Oban, the Naval Control officer had advised all masters that, should you be attacked and sunk and your distress message and position had been sent and acknowledged, then do not attempt any long-distance lifeboat voyage. He said there was always a naval vessel within two days' sailing distance from your position, so just wait for rescue. My chief, who was with Captain Bennett at the conference, confirmed that this was the instruction given.

We waited all through Friday and Saturday, the three boats riding to sea anchors and drifting westwards. Captain Bennett was adamant that we must wait, as it was a Naval Control instruction, but by Saturday evening, the officers rebelled and said that our provisions were limited, so, 'Let's get sailing!' So it was agreed that if no rescue had taken place by Sunday morning, the boats would sail independently for St Vincent, Cape Verde islands.

During these two days, the lifeboat transmitter sent distress messages at regular times, and in particular at the 'silent period' time. Early on Sunday morning, the sea anchors were hauled in and each boat set sail on the prearranged course. By sunset, the chief officer's boat was well ahead, and the second officer's boat was hull-down astern of us. The north-easterly trade winds were blowing steadily, and our speed was estimated at 2.5 to 3 knots. The boat was sailing well, but a good lookout could only be maintained when we rode the crest of the swells.

By Monday morning, both of the other boats were out of sight. At the outset, it was agreed that each boat would sail independently; this would ensure that if one was found by a rescue ship a search could be organised for the other two. It was fine weather and during the day it became very warm; some of the crew were already suffering from sunburn. At night, it was very cold. As the boat was still leaking, it was necessary to bail frequently, but during the day, we would sit with our feet in the water in the hope that our bodies might absorb some moisture this way. Steering the boat was the main task of Captain Bennett and the third officer, although occasionally the other officers would relieve them. Steering at night was difficult as there was no light in the compass. Life jacket lights were used to check the course, but mainly we steered by the stars and moon.

During the next three days, the weather was fine, with fleecy clouds and a strong wind. At times, the sea became choppy, which reduced our speed. When in the valley of a swell one could look up at the side of it and see many varieties of fish swimming above the level of the boat. In this area the sea was a marvellous colour and so clear but, of course, undrinkable.

On Friday – the eighth day – the master estimated that at dawn we had made some 300 miles since setting sail. It was cloudy, and during the morning, there was a light rain shower. The inside cover of the transmitter was used to collect some drops of rain, after which it was licked dry. As thirst was our main problem, Captain Bennett increased our water ration to two and a half dippers a day. On this basis, our stocks should last for another seven days. If our present speed could be maintained, then one of the islands should be sighted before the water ration was exhausted. Ship's biscuits provided for lifeboat use were a disaster, being so dry and hard that no one could eat them. The only food that could be eaten was condensed milk, and the ration of this was increased to two spoonsful a day. Unfortunately, the third officer, who was unwell when we took to the boats, became delirious. In fact, he tried to go overboard but we caught him in time and laid him under the thwarts. He recovered a day or so later.

Monday – 11th day: During the previous few days, the weather had been good and, fortunately, we had remained in the zone of the north-east trades, which enabled us to make a steady speed in spite of a heavy swell. Captain Bennett estimated that by dawn we had sailed about 550 miles, an average speed of 2.5 knots. As we were obviously getting near to the islands, we transmitted distress signals at regular times, but as we had not been supplied with a radio receiver, we did not know if any station was trying to contact us. In the late afternoon, a bird was sighted, which mean that land must be near.

Tuesday – 12th day: It was cloudy and the crew, who were on lookout at dawn, thought that there was a grey smudge on the horizon on our port beam. Could this be an island? If so, then we were some 40 miles off course. The effects of wind and current must have been greater than estimated. This smudge on the horizon was watched by all of us for at least an hour to see if there was any movement – like a dark cloud. It did not move, so it must be one of the islands. The lifeboat's course was now altered to east-north-east, and now we met a headwind, which meant frequent tacking. This gave us severe problems straight away for the sea was rough with quite a swell running.

Shortly after the course had been altered, the heel of the mast broke. It was fixed but we had no tools to carry out a proper repair. It broke again in the forenoon and afternoon, and again was fixed as best as was possible. The boat was being put under severe strain due to the constant tacking and received a great pounding, but fortunately, the mast stays held. While tacking, the boat shipped a lot of water so it was all hands to bailing. Headway was slowly made, and as the day wore on, the island became larger, but by sunset we were still some 20 miles away.

Wednesday – 13th day: I was at the tiller for the night watch; the light at one end of the island was seen and this helped us to maintain a course. The wind dropped and the sea became calmer as we sailed nearer to the island. Later, when some 8 miles from the shore, the master said to me to 'Hold her there'. It was not wise to approach too close to the shore until we could see what it was like. When dawn broke we could make out the layout of the island, and it looked very menacing; the steep, rocky cliffs came down to the sea with no place to land. We sailed in a little closer, and as the sun rose behind the mountains, it began to get very warm. We were now in the lee of the island and the wind dropped completely. For the first time since the *Auditor* sank, our lifeboat was steady and on an even keel. It was now time to ship the oars and row, and as the cliffs looked less steep to the south, that was the way we headed.

Every man took turns at the oars but it was hot and very tiring, particularly as we had not eaten anything substantial for thirteen days. After rowing for three hours, some colours appeared on the mountainside, and these turned out to be the roofs of some small houses. At last, there appeared to be some habitation. Later, we saw two boats making for us; they had brought out two carafes of fresh water. How good it tasted. The boats, manned by local Portuguese fishermen, took our rope and towed us for the last mile or so to the village of Tarrafal on the island of Sao Antão.

Around noon, our boat was brought alongside a stone jetty and we disembarked. How wonderful to walk on the land again. Most of the villagers were there to meet us. The third officer was carried ashore, as were most of the lascars. The remaining survivors walked ashore (although a little unsteadily) and climbed the hillside track to the manager's house, where a room had been made available for us. It was sheer luxury to be able to lay on the floor and relax, with gallons of fresh water available. Captain Bennett warned us not to eat any solid food for several days, as our stomachs would not be able to accept it – and so, the good villagers made us soups. Strange to say, we had arrived at a water-loading terminal. High in the mountains above Tarrafal is a freshwater lake. The Portuguese had piped a supply down to the jetty. Every alternate day, a small tanker arrived and loaded water to take to St Vincent – the capital of the Cape Verde islands. The next day, we would board the tanker to take us to the capital.

On arrival at Tarrafal, the manager of the settlement told us that the second officer's boat had arrived on Monday – two days ahead of us. We were all delighted to hear that his boat had made it, but were intrigued to know how he had beaten us. Apparently, the second officer, who had a steel lifeboat, was very disappointed when, at dusk on the first day's sailing, he was well astern of the other two boats. The next day he found a length of canvas (possibly a boat cover), and from this he made a jib and hoisted it. Fortunately, as he had a steel boat it did not leak and so, with less weight and an extra sail, he made a faster passage.

The next day, just before noon, the water tanker arrived and loaded its cargo of fresh water. We went aboard and sailed at 2.30 p.m., arriving at St Vincent at about 6.00 p.m.

Our lifeboat, which had served us so well during the last two weeks, and which had brought us safely to the island, was left at Tarrafal. News had gone ahead that we were arriving on the water boat. When it docked at the main quay there were not only our chief and second officers with their crews to greet us, but many survivors from the *Clan Macdougall*, the *Silveryew* and a Dutch motor ship.

The chief officer's boat, which had raced ahead of us, had made a good passage. By Tuesday (twelfth day), the islands had not been sighted and so he assumed that they had passed them. He then altered course for the South American coast. This proved to be a good decision, because the next day they were sighted by a Portuguese ship, which brought them and their boat to St Vincent. After the initial wait of two days, all three lifeboats had finally made their objective, the Cape Verde islands.

When discussing our voyages with the other officers they all said that they were very impressed with the performance and seaworthiness of their boats. In hindsight, they should have been better equipped and provisioned, with a larger supply of water. With just the basic equipment of a compass, set of oars, tiller, mast and sail, they had taken severe punishment from heavy swells and choppy seas, but they had completed the voyage. As the name implies, they were indeed lifeboats.

The day after our arrival, Captain Bennett reported to the British Consul and met his staff – all of whom were RN or RNR officers who formed the Naval Control Service for this port. They said that our distress – SSSS – message was received, and after checking their charts, estimated that our boats would arrive in about eleven days' time. When Captain Bennett told them that we had waited two days for rescue (as instructed by Naval Control in Oban), they all burst out laughing and said, 'You can't be serious; we've never heard of that joke before.'

Captain Bennett was so incensed with the Oban Control for issuing such a misguided instruction to shipping that he promptly cabled Harrison's at Liverpool and asked them to lodge a complaint with the Admiralty. Captain Crocker, RN, the Senior Naval Control officer at St Vincent, told Captain Bennett that there were no British naval vessels in the area of the *Auditor*'s sinking, and so there was no hope of any rescue being carried out. It was fortunate that we did not wait any longer and set sail for the islands.

With some 240 merchant seamen at St Vincent, accommodation was at a premium. My chief and I were placed with a local family for a week and then moved to Wilson's, who were T & J Harrison's agents. Their premises had offices on the ground floor and living accommodation on the floor above.

The day after our arrival, we received an advance of pay. This was essential, as we had to visit some shops to buy suitable clothes. Jackets were not available off the peg but had to be made to measure, taking about ten days. Shoes were also made to measure and the local cobbler's turned out a good pair in a few days.

All the *Auditor* survivors made the most of the next few weeks to relax and recover from the ordeal they had been through, the effects of exposure and lack of food and water. The weather was ideal, with blue skies and temperatures in the 70s.

The Cable & Wireless company had a large station at St Vincent, and their staff and families were exceptionally good to survivors. We were invited to their social events, and on occasion were entertained at private dinner parties in their homes. I am certain that their kind hospitality helped us considerably in making a quick and good recovery.

A week after our arrival we said goodbye to the survivors of the *Clan Macdougall*, *Silveryew* and the Dutch ship, who were being repatriated to the UK via Freetown. About that time, we learnt that more survivors had arrived in the port, so we went down to the main quay to greet them. These survivors were from the motor tanker *Horn Shell*, which was torpedoed around the end of July when bound from Gibraltar to Freetown. In charge of lifeboat No. 3 was the second officer, who had a crew of fifteen, which included eleven Chinese. He told us that they had been in the boat for about two weeks when a ship was sighted. It came very near to them and although they shouted and burned flares, it did not stop. Fortunately, the ship's cook came out of the galley to empty a bucket over the side when, on looking aft, he saw their boat. He alerted the mate (who had been asleep on the bridge), and the ship turned back to pick them up. It was a Spanish vessel on passage to the Cape Verde islands.

There was little to do in St Vincent, and to occupy our time we used to go for walks each morning, either around the port, or to the bays and beaches on the other side of the island. The afternoons were spent resting, and in the early evening most of us went to the Plaza to walk around this large square. It appeared that half the town's population carried this ritual each evening, using the occasion to chat with friends and relatives before going home to an evening meal.

During the morning walks, I found it was difficult for me to face the bright sunlight. Even using a pair of dark glasses did not improve my sight. Captain Bennett thought I should see a specialist (there were no special facilities in St Vincent), and the agents arranged for me to be sent to Lisbon to go into the British Hospital and possibly see an ophthalmic surgeon.

It was Friday, 19 August that we had another unusual event. I was awakened about 4.00 a.m. by rumbling noises, only to find my washbasin dancing around the marble-topped table. I suddenly realised that St Vincent was being hit by an earthquake. I quickly got out of bed and ran down the outside stairs to the quadrangle below. All the other people in the building did the same thing, and we waited there until the earthquake had subsided. Apparently, it was not too severe, and there was only superficial damage. However, I well remember the streetlights swinging to and fro, and wondering if Wilson's building might collapse.

A few days later, I was told that a passage had been booked for me and the chief steward of the *Auditor* in the Portuguese liner *Serpa Pinto*, 8,489 tons, which was calling at St Vincent next weekend en route to Lisbon. (Incidentally, the *Serpa Pinto* was built for Royal Mail Lines in 1915 as the *Ebro*. The Portuguese shipping company Cia Colonial of Lisbon purchased her in 1940 for their New York and Central American Service. As Portugal was neutral, it was essential to have her name and country in very large letters on each side of the ship.)

On Saturday, 23 August, five weeks after arriving in the islands, I said farewell to the *Auditor*'s crew, and with the chief steward embarked in the *Serpa Pinto*. The second officer and third engineer of the *Horn Shell* also joined us, as their company – Anglo Saxon Petroleum – were repatriating them to the UK via Lisbon. We sailed early next morning, calling at Madeira on Wednesday, and arrived at Lisbon late on Friday evening.

At night, the *Serpa Pinto* was floodlit so that any U-boat sighting her knew it was a neutral ship. There had been one or two occasions previously when she had been stopped and searched. In fact, in early 1941 she had been stopped by the British and ordered into Bermuda, where a three-day search was carried out for Germans believed to have been aboard. Fortunately for us, she was not stopped on this voyage.

Although the *Serpa Pinto* had accommodation for some 500 1st and 2nd class passengers, she was not fully booked for her return voyage to Lisbon. One of her passengers was a British Consulate inspector who was returning from a South American tour of duty. The four of us got to know him quite well, and it transpired that his relations lived very near to my home in Essex. On arrival at Lisbon, we were met by a consulate, who cleared us through immigration and customs in record time, and took us to the Bragança Hotel in the centre of the city.

The next day, the same official called early and took me to the British Hospital, where I was examined and arrangements were made for me to see an eye specialist later that day. The same official came with me and stayed for a long time to interpret, as I could not speak Portuguese. He left me with the specialist, who worked on my eye during the next eight days. I stayed at his surgery during the day and he would call me in several times to give me treatment. I found out later that I had corneal ulcers, which the specialist had been able to disperse, and so saved my sight.

With my sight greatly improved, the chief steward and I reported daily to the British Consulate to check if they could arrange repatriation for us to the UK. There was a possibility that we could be flown back, but at the last minute, it was cancelled due to other people having greater priority. On Monday, 15 September, I was asked to call at the Consulate and was told that a Danish ship, the SS *Ebro*, required a radio officer for a voyage to the UK. As I wanted to return home as soon as possible, either working or as a DBS [Distressed British Seaman], I accepted and signed on. The Consulate also arranged for the chief steward to return to Liverpool as a passenger in the SS *Cortes*.

The *Ebro* (1,600 tons) had just completed loading a cargo of cork when I joined her. Shortly after my arrival, a lady and her two children came aboard; they were the only passengers, as this ship had very limited accommodation. A Scottish engineer, whose ship had been torpedoed, had reached Lisbon by a roundabout route and also joined as third engineer. Prior to the war, the *Ebro* had been sailing on short-sea voyages, mainly from the Baltic to the Mediterranean.

Leaving Lisbon at dusk, we hugged the Portuguese coast that night and all next day, arriving at Gibraltar at 3.00 p.m. As we were entering port, a convoy of twenty-four ships was leaving. Hardly had we anchored in the bay when a launch came alongside and a Naval Control officer came aboard. He instructed us to join Convoy HG 73, which had just sailed, and briefed us on the operational procedures and gave us a convoy plan. As the *Ebro* had a good turn of speed, we had no trouble catching up with this convoy. We were allotted position No. 54, the third ship astern of the commodore. I was instructed to discontinue normal radio watches and to assist the master (Danish) and the two deck officers (one Danish, the other Norwegian) with convoy instructions and signalling with the Aldis lamp and flags.

Chapter Seven

The DEMS Gunners

The training of Merchant Navy personnel to handle the armament of their ships had begun some twelve months before the outbreak of the Second World War, but it soon became obvious that outside help was needed, and in June 1939, the Defensively Equipped Merchant Ships (DEMS) organisation was formed. This consisted of experienced gunners from the Royal Navy and the Royal Artillery who were allocated to merchantmen, up to ten men per ship, depending on the number of guns. As maritime nations on the Continent came under the yoke of Germany, any of their ships that were able to escape to British ports were also similarly armed and manned. In their ranks was Rotterdam South America Line's 5,483-ton motor vessel *Alioth*. Sergeant E.G. Robson of the Maritime Regiment, Royal Artillery, senior DEMS gunner of the *Alioth*, has this tale to tell:

In May 1942, I was a bombardier in the 5th Maritime Regiment, Royal Artillery. I joined a Dutch ship, the m.v. *Alioth*, at Liverpool, and was in charge of four gunners from my regiment. They were Wally Harding, Dan Hawes, Jim Darby and 'Toffee' Tomkinson, so called because of his 'toffee-nosed' appearance. The ship was loaded with landmines, bombs, ammunition and various other military stores destined for Iraq, and a deck cargo of Anson aircraft for Cape Town.

The ship's armament consisted of two Lewis guns, which we brought on board and mounted each side of the boat deck, two Hotchkiss machine guns mounted in gun pits each side of the bridge, a 12-pounder HA/LA gun mounted aft, and a 4-inch surface gun on the stern.

To man this equipment, we were five MRA gunners, a leading seaman and two ordinary seamen RN. We got on very well together and soon became a happy crew. The Merchant Navy crew on board were all Dutch, with the exception of one of the engineers, who was Belgian, and two deck boys and two seamen who were from Liverpool. So you can see that the British were very much in the minority, but we got on very well with the crew, and in particular the Belgian engineer. It was his job to attend to the small diesel engine in the No. 1 lifeboat. He would turn that engine over every day, and ensured that it was kept in good running order – for which we were to be very thankful in the weeks to come!

We sailed from Liverpool in late May 1942, joined the main convoy north of Ireland in pouring rain, and sailed south. We kept aircraft watch until we were out of aircraft range, and eventually cleared the bad weather and enjoyed some sunshine. A Sunderland flying boat circling the convoy was a comforting sight until its departure for England, while we ploughed on with the convoy until it altered course for Gibraltar and we continued on a southerly course for South Africa. Being a fast ship, it was assumed that we could make the passage on our own, and that by keeping a good lookout and zigzagging, we would be able to avoid any U-boats.

We settled down to the ship routine, working one watch on and two off. When on watch we kept a strict lookout, but apart from the odd wisp of smoke on the horizon and one topmast, the only ship that we came upon was a Portuguese vessel with all lights blazing, and clearly identifiable.

When off watch we had normal maintenance of our guns and ammunition, plus, of course, our domestic chores, such as the cleanliness of our accommodation, feeding, washing up and dhobying to attend to. Our recreational period was always during the dog watches, which were passed in the usual shipboard manner with cards, reading or exchanging the current galley wireless news, and such like.

We did have a small monkey on board, owned by one of the engineers. This was a source of entertainment, until it fell out of favour by biting the first mate. The monkey was henceforth banished to the paint locker ... and went down with the ship, which was a better fate than being eaten by the crew.

On the evening of 10 June, we had played pontoon with some of the crew. At about nine o'clock, having made myself a cup of very sweet cocoa with condensed milk and sugar, I also made a cheese and pickle sandwich and then turned into my bunk for a couple of hours before turning out again for the middle watch with Wally. Before getting into my bunk, I ensured that my panic bag was to hand. My panic bag consisted of my Army-issue haversack, inside of which was an oilskin wallet with my Army pay book, wallet and money, together with a few articles of clothing such as spare trousers and a blazer, which I thought might come in handy.

Sometime around 10.00 p.m., there was an almighty explosion and Dan and his bunk collapsed on top of me. For what seemed like an eternity, I struggled to free myself. There were no lights ... not until someone produced a torch. I grabbed my panic bag and somehow found my way up on deck. All the men who had been in the cabin had got out, and I saw one of the naval gunners running stark naked towards the boat deck carrying a large suitcase. I started to make my way to the gun deck aft, but one of the gunners who had been on watch told me that the order had been given to abandon ship. The ship was by then settling by the stern, and I thought at first that we had been in collision with something, reasoning that a torpedo hit would have set off our cargo of ammunition. It eventually transpired that we had been hit by a torpedo low down on the propeller shaft, under the only hold that did not contain ammunition. Just how lucky can one be in such circumstances?

Having had frequent boat drills, the whole crew knew exactly where to go and what to do, so lifeboats and scrambling nets were already being lowered. The chief steward appeared with a large wooden case, later found to contain tins of Carnation milk. He placed it into one of the lifeboats before it was lowered.

By this time, the enemy submarine had surfaced and taken up position ahead of us, where it knew it was safe. (At that time in the war, merchant ships had no armaments mounted forward of the bridge. Under the international law governing war at sea, this would have been classified as offensive armament.) We could not therefore take any retaliatory action when the enemy submarine opened fire on us to hasten our departure from the sinking ship.

There was a very heavy swell running when it came my turn to down the scrambling net, and I can remember losing my grip with my left hand and thinking that I had pulled my right arm off – which today, still gives me some trouble. Following me came the bosun with one small deck boy. Apparently, the bosun had gone aft to get his wallet and had found the deck boy still fast asleep in his bunk. It had taken him some time to rouse the boy and drag him, still half asleep, to the boat deck. Later, the bosun realised that in his concern for the boy, he had forgotten his wallet.

We had cast off and rowed as best we could to get away from the ship. The starboard lifeboat had also cast off, and having got the engine running, came around and took us in tow to clear the ship, which was by now undergoing intensive gunfire from the submarine. We were all in hope of them setting off the cargo of landmines and bombs, blowing themselves up in the process, but either their gunnery was rotten or the *Alioth* sank from the effects of the torpedo hit.

As we expected the submarine to catch us up, I ordered all my gunners to hide what uniform they were wearing, as none of us relished the prospect of a trip in a submarine, let alone being a POW. I had all my civilian gear in my panic bag, and as I was only wearing a vest, PT shorts and slippers, was not feeling too warm. We then found that Wally Harding must have been in a state of shock. He had only his PT shorts on and did not have his panic bag with him, so to keep him warm we lent him two pullovers. One he wore on his upper torso, and the other we managed, with some difficulty, to get onto the lower portion of his body. He cut a very fine figure.

The lifeboat was getting very waterlogged, which was quite to be expected, as all the timbers had dried out while the boat was out of the water. We were kept busy with bailing cans until the timbers had taken up. We were all very seasick that first night – again something to be expected, with the change from the gentle motion of a well-founded ship to the pitching and tossing of a small boat in a large sea. When dawn broke, we came alongside the No. 1 boat and took stock of our situation, and then planned our tactics to survive. There were twenty-two of the crew in our boat and twenty in the other, but because of the engine in their boat, they were rather cramped for space. It was decided that the engine in No. 1 boat would only be used in an emergency, or at night to keep headway on both boats, and so maintain our correct course.

So, having decided on such matters as the course to be set and routine to be adopted, we shared out the case of milk between the two boats, hoisted sail, and got underway. Our boat being the lighter of the two took the lead, and kept station about a mile ahead of No. 1. Before dusk each evening, No. 1 would start its engine, catch us up, and take us in tow until dawn the next day. This was the drill each day, and that lovely little engine never let us down.

In charge of our boat was the chief mate, and amongst the remainder were the second officer, third officer, chief engineer, a sparks, an assistant steward, various deck and engine room crew, the two O/Ss, RN gunners, and my four gunners. Once the boat had stopped leaking, we made ourselves as comfortable as was possible by fixing an awning over the forward end of the boat, and with the floorboards and oars rigged a flat area. This made quite a snug cuddy where the watch below could get some sleep. We had by now been split into three watches, which meant we did four hours sailing and keeping lookout, four hours sitting amidships, and four hours in the cuddy trying to get some sleep. Blankets were on hand and were much needed when the temperature plunged at night. Some parts of the cuddy were more comfortable than others, so we moved a place at each sleep watch. Thanks to the second officer, we became very well organised. He had taken over from the chief officer, who was much older and had become ill.

The naked sailor I had seen running for the boat with his suitcase still had the case with him. It was full of clothing, which was shared amongst those not so well off. Wally Harding was able to doff his two pullovers and was attired in trousers and a shirt to protect him from the sun. Another seaman had a small case with him, which contained his stock of cigarettes in fifty tins. These were put into the kitty and rationed out to two fags each morning, afternoon and evening to each person on board. When these ran out after six days, my pouch of tobacco (I had lost my pipe in the rush to leave the ship) was taken over and made into cigarettes.

We had three containers of water: one small keg in which the water was dirty, one tank of rusty water, and one of clean water. The rusty water was OK after you left the rust to settle. We only had three cups for drinking out of, but as we emptied the cigarette tins, they were used, and you then had your own mug with a lid in which you could save your water and sip it slowly to stave off thirst pangs. Water was rationed out twice a day, morning and evening, and the ration amounted to about half an inch in a fifty-fag tin – not a lot on, or near, the equator under a blazing sun, but it was nectar.

For solids, we had two concentrated oatmeal biscuits a day and there was also some really hard old tack ship's biscuits, very dry and the last sort of food one could eat when so deprived of liquids. The second steward found a 7lb tin of corned beef amongst the stores, a real luxury, but of course there was no opener, so my Army-issue jackknife came into use for this, and also for the milk. After each time of using, it was religiously returned to me, and I still have it in use today. Having opened the corned beef, we had to eat the lot, as in that temperature it would have gone off. Have you ever eaten warm corned beef out of your not-too-clean hands, which had been given to you by hands that were also not too clean? I can assure you that not a crumb was wasted. This feast took place on the fourth day. We got a ration of Carnation milk each day, and although this was sustaining, it made one thirsty.

Part of my gear was a blue blazer, which had black wooden buttons, and one of the apprentices asked me for one to suck as it would help to keep his mouth moist. I followed suit, and it certainly helped, but five minutes later, a very apologetic apprentice asked for another button, as he had absent-mindedly chewed the button and swallowed it. So my three buttons disappeared in a good cause, as also did my cuff buttons.

Sanitary arrangements were solved by using a small bucket, which was emptied over the side, but as our liquid intake was limited, so was our output, which was very discoloured and painful. As for passing solids, one member did get concerned about this, and after his very painful experience, nobody else bothered.

It is difficult to recollect events in chronological order, but one day we were becalmed for the whole of the day in a metallic haze. We could not see the sun and the sea was like a sheet of glass and the heat unbearable.

That evening, it was our turn off watch in the cuddy, when we were roused by a very fierce wind, and we seemed to be heading for tall black cliffs when suddenly the wind changed and we were forced to down sails and get out the oars to bring us around. I was on an oar with a big beefy second cook and seemed to spend more time in the air than on the seat! It was a nightmare, but we got her around with a struggle, and the other boat got a line over to us. During the nights, we festooned the mast and sails with the small red battery operated lights from our life jackets so that we could be seen by any passing vessel, and they looked nice and cheered us up.

Shortly after the above incident, we hit the mother and father of a tropical storm, with waves as big as a house. I do not know to this day which was the worst, being on top of such a wave and looking down, or being in the trough and looking up at the wall of water, which you are sure is going to swamp you. I cannot remember much about the wind, except that it was a continuous roar and the lightning, both sheet and forked, played around us, with St Elmo's fire in the rigging. The rain hit us in squalls, and I have never been so wet in all my life – that storm put a new dimension to the word 'scared'. When the storm had passed and the rain fell steadily for hours, we collected water in sheets, and refilled all our by now empty containers. From being hydrated we were now waterlogged, and everything was soaked – clothing, life jackets and blankets.

Dawn broke to grey clouds and the sea running a swell, but it was now our turn to bed down in the cuddy, which we did in spite of all our clothing and blankets being saturated. We were wet and warm, and stayed that way, unlike one member, who decided to strip off and wrap himself in a wet blanket, and who could not stop shivering for two hours.

We spent most of our time talking, reminiscing and planning our futures. We all said we would never go back to sea again and would transfer out, but as it turned out, we all went back. The Dutch officers jokingly promoted me to sergeant, and when I did get back to my regiment I was promoted to lance sergeant, but I doubt if the Dutch officers had anything to do with it. Food, or rather the lack of it, did not seem to bother us a great deal, even though the cook described the feast he would cook for us when we were rescued, but talk of a nice foaming glass of cold beer was agony. The sea always looked tempting enough to drink, but no one succumbed, though we did trail our arms in the water, also our feet, in an attempt to absorb some moisture into our dried-up bodies.

We were sailing on a course that should have taken us to Freetown, with the mates bringing out their sextants each day for a midday shot of the sun, and setting our course allowing for drift, etc. I and the others in the boat owe our lives to those Dutchmen, and I will be eternally grateful to them for the way in which they organised the boats, and for their disciplined and skilful navigation.

We had our lighter moments, such as the day we had a steady light rain storm that seemed to come from nowhere. Most of us stripped off and let the shower soak into us. It was not enough to catch for drinking, but we must have looked a fine sight. It was a pity we had no camera handy. The two Scouse seamen pulled a tarpaulin over their heads to keep dry. They must have been Liverpool-Irish!

By this time, our biscuits were running low, but we had a box of very stale chocolates – one each was the ration. The condensed milk was also running to a low level. In fact, everything was dwindling, except our hopes. I suppose everyone prayed in their own way. I did, and was convinced that my prayers were being heard. I cannot even now explain the feeling, but it was like throwing a dart at a dartboard and knowing that at the very moment the dart leaves your hand that it is going to hit the bullseye. I have never felt the same with prayer since, though I am still a great believer in it. The answer these days seems to be 'NO'.

On the eighth day, we began to see signs of floating vegetation and a few sea birds appeared, a sure sign of nearing land, and we were also getting frequent tropical rainstorms, with visibility almost nil. We now had plenty of water, in fact more than we needed, and I remember the chief engineer courteously offering me a tin full to the brim with water and myself, in a like vein, politely refusing it. A couple of days previously, such an action would have been impossible.

During the evening of the ninth day, the motor lifeboat caught up with us, and passing us a line began their usual night tow when, as darkness descended, there was a shout from a lookout that a light was flashing dead ahead. The mates said it was possibly Freetown, to which they had been plotting our course, but that it could also be Dakar, which was being held by the Vichy French. That being the case, it was their intention to make a sharp alteration to our course, as none of us wished to be interned in Dakar for the remainder of the war.

I came off watch at 4.00 a.m. and was then violently awakened as dawn broke with a whole tin of Carnation milk in my hand. Half asleep, and very bemused, I started protesting vigorously at having my head turned round, then saw that we were sailing along a coastline. It was Freetown and we were going through the boom. We were still being towed, but at 4 knots against a 9-knot tide. We were not getting anywhere fast. However, we had not given up hope, as there were plenty of other craft about; if not within hailing distance, they were near enough to see us. There were also plenty of aircraft around. We whistled and did our best to shout, but to no avail. Nobody was in the least interested in us. Then the rain descended once again and blotted us from view as visibility became nil.

After a while, and it is difficult to say how long, to our horror there was an aircraft carrier coming at us out of the rain at the speed of an express train. After all we had gone through we were going to be drowned; after ten days of suffering trials and tribulations, only to be finished off by the Royal Navy. Didn't they know it was their job to rescue and care for us poor merchant seamen types? This was the only moment in the whole ten days when something like panic seemed very near, and resulted in me having a tug of war over a life jacket with one of the RN gunners.

Afterwards, neither could really say whose jacket it was, and we never did find out, as at the very last minute, the carrier altered course and missed us. We later heard that they were calling us a lot of rude names, as they thought we were native fishermen in a prohibited area, and it was only by good luck that their lookouts had spotted us for what we really were.

It was not long before we were aboard the carrier, which proved to be HMS *Archer*, an escort carrier converted from a former Italian liner. She was not rated to be a lucky ship. The day before she picked us up, when bombing up a Swordfish aircraft, one of the bombs had gone off, killing six of the crew and injuring many more, so their medical department was rather too busy to give us much attention. I was the first to board the *Archer*, and as soon as I touched the deck, my legs gave under me. However, two burly matelots grabbed me and took me below, followed by the remainder of our survivors.

The crew of the *Archer* were marvellous; they loaned us shaving kit, soap and towels and took us to the showers. Absolute bliss, and I just wanted to stay under that shower for ever. Having been cleaned up, we donned what was left of our clothing and they brought us trays of food. I felt that perhaps we should not eat so much after ten days on a starvation diet, but with no doctor to guide us – and I doubt if we would have paid much heed if we did have one – we fell to on the generous helping of eggs, bacon, sausages, fried bread, tomatoes, bread and butter. In fact, the whole lot went down in no time at all, washed down with gallons of nice hot coffee. God, what a feast! It was the finest meal I have ever had, before or since. We really enjoyed it … and no after effects.

After the usual service period of hurry up and wait, we were taken ashore. Then began the usual questioning after such an event by a commander RNVR, who seemed to take a very dim view of us and thought we should have stayed on the *Alioth* and gone down fighting with the ship. A fat lot of good that would have done the war effort. The *Alioth* was doomed the moment that torpedo smashed its propeller shaft. Anyhow, the said commander RNVR had in all probability never been in a position to take such a decision for himself. Desks don't get torpedoed!

After this interesting episode we were transported to a transit camp in the hills above Freetown, a journey almost as hazardous as the ten days in the boats, though thankfully not so long. After a visit to the meanest quartermaster I had ever met, who issued us with the minimum of our requirements, we had once again to face questioning and had further reports to make out. This was followed by a visit to the MO, who could find very little wrong with us, apart from our feet, which were swollen and soft, with the skin coming off them, for which he prescribed treatment that, apart from turning our grey Army socks a bright yellow, did little else. Although we were excused boots, we did cut quite a dash amongst the rest of the military long before such fashions were in vogue.

The remainder of the story is a mixture of bumbledom and sheer military stupidity. The army in Freetown found a captain of a merchant ship who was willing to have us work our passage back as gunners. Of course, we were not told the ship was a tanker; that was left for us to find out on the day we were to join her. We did protest, but to no avail. We were not too hard done by, as she was not carrying aviation spirit, only crude oil. We decided that maybe it was in any case better than stinking Freetown. So five very reluctant gunners made their way to the UK on a tanker, with little hope for the future.

Do you know, I cannot even now remember the name of that ship, and I remember very little of the voyage home, except that we lived in our life jackets until we were finally put ashore in Greenock. There we were issued with battledress, but no caps, and put aboard a train for London. I was still wearing my PT shorts as underpants, and had no vest, so my new shirt and battledress irritated like hell and I spent a very uncomfortable journey to Euston. From there it was to Fenchurch Street station for the final leg back to Shoeburyness, where after the usual documentation and further questions, we were kitted out completely. We also received £10 each from the survivors' fund to assist in the replacement of personal items lost.

We stowed our gear in the QM's stores and went on our fourteen days' survivor's leave, and of course when I arrived home, my mother and dad were very surprised, as they had expected me to be away for at least a year. I think Dad was very proud of me by the way he talked about me to his pals at the Lord Napier. I didn't feel proud – just bloody glad to be alive and well. I had not done anything wonderful – except survive.

Chapter Eight

An Eventful Voyage

By the time the First World War drew to a close in the winter of 1918, Britain's merchant fleet was severely depleted, mainly because of German U-boat activity. Consequently, as soon as hostilities ended, British shipyards were busy turning out replacement vessels. One of these was the 6,445-ton, refrigerated *War Peony*, a product of Napier & Miller on the Clyde.

The *War Peony* went to Lord Vestey's Blue Star Line to replace one of the four ships the company had lost during the war. She was renamed *Lusiada*, and later became the *Viking Star*, spending the years between the wars carrying frozen beef to the UK from Vestey's ranches in Argentina. When Able Seaman Stan Mayes joined her in 1942, she was a vital link in Britain's transatlantic food chain.

After paying off the *San Emiliano*, I had a few days' leave and then attended a gunnery course given on HMS *Chrysanthemum*, which was moored on the Thames in London. These courses for machine guns and small arms lasted five days and were followed by another three days' instruction for 4-inch and 12-pounder guns.

This second course took place at Sheerness, and when completed I received a Merchant Navy gunnery certificate entitling me to 6*d* per day while I was signed on ship's articles.

During this period, very few deep-sea ships came into London, and as I did not care to sail on coasters or colliers, I would go to Liverpool or Glasgow, where there was a choice of ships.

This time I went to Liverpool and found accommodation in the Angel Club in Dale Street. This was a hotel run by the Flying Angel Mission to Seafarers.

I spent three days there and then signed on the *Viking Star* of the Blue Star Line of London. The voyage was from 21 May to mid-October 1942. In convoy from the Mersey, we later joined in with other ships from the Clyde and sailed around Northern Ireland and into the Atlantic, bound for Freetown, West Africa. Apart from an unsuccessful attack on the ships by two Focke-Wulf aircraft, the ten-day voyage was uneventful. We spent two days at anchor at Freetown, which was a large convoy port. We then sailed in a convoy that was dispersed twenty-four hours later with all ships sailing independently to their various destinations, ours being the Argentine.

Torpedoed

With the *Viking Star* making only 10 knots, we had an uneventful twenty-five days' voyage, seeing only one other ship – the large American sailing ship *Tango*, which was bound from Panama for Cape Town. At Buenos Aires, we discharged our general cargo, which included four racehorses that were in wooden stalls stowed on the main deck.

While in Buenos Aires, we had a serious fire in the ship's paint store, caused by saboteurs who were sympathetic to the German cause. Other Allied ships suffered sabotage also. Many of the crew of the *Graf Spee*, who had been interned in Uruguay for a time after scuttling their ship off Montevideo, were now living in Argentina. They had elected to live there rather than return home to Germany.

Another memory of Buenos Aires is that, in conversation with the padre of the Seaman's Club and telling him I was from Grays, he told me he had recently conducted a burial service for a lad from Grays who had been killed when falling into the hold of the Royal Mail Line's *Nagara*. The lad, Harry Barrell, was well known to me as being the son of the publican of The Theobald Arms in Grays High Street. The padre gave me a photo of the grave to take home to his parents, but they never received it as it went down with my ship about four weeks later. I also lost a ring my parents gave me for my twenty-first birthday and had presented to me before sailing.

With repairs completed, *Viking Star* loaded 6,000 tons of meat and sailed for Montevideo at the end of July. At that port, we loaded 1,000 tons of fertilisers and our destination was the UK. The wreck of the *Graf Spee* lay outside Montevideo.

Sailing from Montevideo, our voyage was uneventful until the morning of 25 August, when a Sunderland flying boat circled the ship three times. In spite of trying to make contact with the Aldis lamp, we received no reply. Eventually, the aircraft departed.

At 1645 hours on the same day, we were in position 0600N 1400W, and about 200 miles south-west of Freetown. Two torpedoes struck the ship on the port side amidships, throwing a tremendous column of water into the air and over the bridge. The two lifeboats on the port side were demolished by the explosion, derricks were smashed and covers were blown off the bunker hatch. At the time, I was in my cabin aft and the explosions caused the ship to shudder violently. All the lights went out, so in total darkness and with much shouting we found our way to the companionway leading up to the deck. Running along the deck to the lifeboats, we were showered by falling debris thrown into the air by the explosions.

No. 1 lifeboat, on the starboard side, was damaged by being lowered, and filled with water as it met the sea. Her occupants swam over to our No. 3 boat as soon as we had launched. Only one boat from the four carried on the ship was sound. Eight life rafts were also released from the ship. These rafts were constructed from timber boards and a dozen empty 40-gallon drums, but were the means of saving countless lives. Lockers were built into them for the storage of water and provisions. The captain, with two other crew, took to one of the rafts and soon drifted astern as the ship was still moving ahead, although rapidly sinking. On launching the one sound boat, we began taking men from the sea until we could embark no more for fear of sinking. The boat was designed for twenty-eight persons and we had thirty-six aboard. We then assisted other men in the sea to get onto drifting rafts – thirteen men in all. More survivors were already on other rafts in the distance. Five of the crew had been killed on the ship.

By this time, the *Viking Star* had sunk to deck level, and as the last man climbed onto a raft another torpedo struck the ship, and this caused her to break her back. With bows and stern pointing to the sky, she sank in the shape of a huge V. From the first torpedo to her end was less than fifteen minutes, and indeed, it was a very sad sight to behold.

A few minutes later, the U-boat surfaced, and on approaching us we were asked if any officers were among us. To this, we replied they were all lost with the ship. The chief and second officers were in the lifeboat and the third officer was on a raft, but none of them was wearing uniform. Among the crew of the U-boat in her conning tower was her captain, a tall man with a red beard – now known to be Commander Ernst Kals. The U-boat was *U-130*. Photos were taken of us in the boat and on the rafts, and then the U-boat departed. Some hours later, *U-130* torpedoed and sank another British ship, the *Beechwood*, of John I. Jacobs.

Soon we were surrounded by many sharks and barracudas, who were after the sides of beef coming to the surface from our sunken ship. We moored the boat to the two rafts and lay as such throughout the night. Occasionally, we fired off a distress flare in the hopes of it being seen by a passing ship and our flares were replied to by flares from the captain's raft, which was about 5 miles distant. After the first night they were never seen alive again.

At dawn, we hoisted sail and attempted to tow the rafts, but it proved futile. The boat, which was of wooden construction, was leaking badly and had only 14 inches of freeboard above water. During the day, a discussion was held with the men on the rafts and it was suggested that we sail to the coast and have help sent to them. We were asked to remain until the following day, to which we readily agreed.

During the night, the wind blew hard and caused a choppy sea, and water began slopping inboard. We removed it by some frantic bailing. Also, the rafts were bumping together uncomfortably. Next morning, the question of separating was raised again and agreed on. So we passed over some extra stores, water and blankets. I then witnessed a very heroic act by Able Seaman J. Daintith. He gave up his place in the lifeboat to DEMS Gunner Hancock from the water-logged raft, knowing he would have far less chance of survival – or none at all in the shark-infested seas.

Hoisting sail, we departed and from then on, the bosun and I steered the boat, as we both had sailboat experience – mine being in Thames sailing barges from the London river to the east coast and Channel ports for four years and six months.

Torpedoed and adrift

We had four hours on and four hours off at the tiller, while the other men were on a rota in bailing out water from the leaking boat. They used a bailer (large metal scoop) and empty condensed milk tins. We steered by the sun and the stars, as we had no other means of navigation – our lifeboat compass had been stolen in Buenos Aires or Montevideo. We were constantly accompanied by sharks and barracudas, which at times came too close for comfort. We also saw many manatees and large stingrays. All hands suffered severely from sunburn as little clothing was worn by any of us. We were rationed to two pieces of chocolate in the morning with 2oz of water. At midday, we had two biscuits with pemmican and another 2 oz of water. In the evening, we had chocolate and malted milk tablets. With so many men in the boat and with little space, some had their legs across the legs of others, and to add to our discomfort, during the hours of darkness it was very cold.

Some hours after leaving the rafts, a dispute began among the men bailing out water, and in an attempt to settle the problem the bosun was struck in one eye with the metal bailer, causing a serious injury. So I remained at the tiller for the following thirty hours. For this I later received a commendation from Chief Officer McQuisto. The row was caused by two or three of the men avoiding their turn on the rota in bailing out, and it seems incredible that such a thing could occur when we were fighting for survival against the sea and in the vicinity of so many sharks. But such was the apathy of some of those men.

Late one evening we realised we were nearing the land, as there was a different motion to the sea. The long steep rollers had become short choppy waves, which frequently slopped over the sides of the boat and caused some frantic bailing out. Soon we were in big breakers, so we lowered the sail and attempted to turn the boat seaward with the oars. But our efforts were to no avail and in minutes the boat was overwhelmed by the seas and capsized, throwing everybody into the seething surf. There then followed a desperate struggle for survival, but survive we did. The time was about 0400 hours on 29 August 1942.

Struggling from the surf and reaching the beach safely, we found it to be very cold so we began to salvage the mast and sail with the intention of erecting a shelter against the biting wind.

On completing this job, we spotted a native, who ran away when we called to him, but he soon returned with many others. Among them was a young native girl who told us she was a missionary and had been trained in Freetown. She informed us we were in Sierra Leone, close to the Liberian border.

We were very fortunate in having had a following wind from the south-west while sailing the boat, as we could not have sailed against the wind under the prevailing conditions. We would therefore have had many more days adrift, unless we had been seen by a passing ship.

The missionary explained to her people who we were and then took us to a nearby village where we were given food and later entered mud huts to sleep for a while. A few hours later, we left the village and walked through the jungle in single file, escorted by the natives until we reached another village. Here we stayed overnight in mud huts, and the following day we walked to yet another village, again escorted by the natives, who walked on either side of us clearing the way of snakes and wild animals, of which we saw many. From this village, a native went to Bonthe to report to the district commissioner, who lived there. Later, we travelled across swamps in canoes to two launches that had been sent to rescue us.

We were then taken many miles down a river to Bonthe (now called Sherbro), and on arrival here we were accommodated with British and Swiss traders who resided there. These traders exchanged clothing, knives, tobacco and trinkets with the natives for animal hides, horns and snakeskins. Also, groundnuts were produced here and stored in a large shed. These were later loaded into a small ship, which called on occasion and took the cargo to Freetown.

A radio message was sent to Freetown, and two days later, an MTB arrived and took us all to Freetown, where we entered hospital suffering with malaria and other tropical diseases. At the time, Freetown was a large convoy port and naval base, and an ex-Union Castle liner was moored there and in use as an accommodation ship. This was the *Edinburgh Castle*. Also based there and in use as an RN repair ship was the *Philoctetes* of Blue Funnel Line, and the *City of Tokyo*, of Ellerman Lines.

On arrival at Freetown, we had been informed that telegrams had been sent to our next of kin. A ship missing with crew presumed dead was the *Viking Star*, which had been due in Freetown on the day after her sinking. It was now about ten days later.

After a few days in hospital, some of us were released and accommodated in a native school, which had been taken over for this purpose. More than a hundred other survivors from sunken ships were already accommodated there, and each man had a cot bed protected by mosquito netting. We were also fitted out with new clothing and shoes. We spent two days in the school and then boarded the Orient Line's troopship *Otranto*, which had arrived from Cape Town. She later sailed indepenently for the UK. Already on board the *Otranto* were survivors from the *Tuscan Star*, which had been torpedoed and sunk on 6 September by *U-109*. The *Otranto* had sighted their lifeboat and rescued them the day after the sinking. Two other lifeboats with survivors sailed into the coast of Liberia.

The day we sailed from Freetown in the *Otranto* we were told that the survivors who had been on the rafts had made landfall in Liberia, some 40 miles beyond our landing place. They had abandoned one raft and using a blanket as a sail had made the land in twelve days. Unfortunately, a DEMS gunner lost his life when the raft capsized in heavy surf.

At the time of this sinking I was an able seaman and my monthly pay was £22 12s 6d. Of this, £10 12s 6d was paid by the shipowner and £12 per month was war bonus, or war risk money, which was paid by the Government. From the day a ship was lost, all wages for the crew ceased, as in my case, and was only paid again on my arrival in the UK, when I reported myself as being alive to Tilbury Shipping Office. My pay from Blue Star Line was backdated to the day of the sinking, and paid until my arrival in Liverpool. The next of kin of seamen who lost their lives received no payment.

From that day in 1942, I have met only one other survivor from the *Viking Star*. He was Cliff Maw, the deck boy on his first voyage. We sailed together in the tanker *Dolabella* and saw three months' service on the beachheads during the Normandy operations. I was in correspondence with Captain Rigiani for a number of years. He was third officer of the ship and was in charge of the rafts. He was master of a Blue Star liner in 1967 when he heard I was working as a rigger in Tilbury Docks, and he contacted me by letter through my office. In later years, he became shore superintendent of Blue Star Line in Liverpool. On retirement, he went to live in Chicago. Sadly, he passed away in 1994.

One by one, the dwindling number of Second World War survivors fade away, and all that will be left will be the names and words in history books, as no longer will there be men and women who speak of those terrible times at sea. Ships – these floating masses of metal that in years gone by we called homes. Some of these ships were like a second home, and a good crew were like another family.

Good old days? There will never again ever be so much camaraderie in the seafaring world as we experienced, and I feel privileged in having shared those experiences and the camaraderie. To write these memories is a vanity with a purpose, as maybe one day my grandchildren will ask the question: 'What did Granddad do in his life?'

Chapter Nine

The Deliverance

Built on the Tees in 1919, the 5,221-ton *Peterton* was a typical North East Coast tramp, one of Chapman's of Newcastle-upon-Tyne, and being thus, she carried a typical tramp's cargo – 5,758 tons of best steaming coal from the mines of the North East. Not that her cargo mattered to Heinrich Bleichrodt as he viewed her through his periscope. She was just another target to add to his mounting toll of Allied shipping. In the six patrols he had been in command of the long-range boat *U-109*, he had accounted for 80,000 tons. When the *Peterton* and her cargo lay on the bottom, it was time to go home.

The story of the *Peterton*'s loss and the subsequent fate of her survivors is taken from the diary of First Radio Officer Johnathan Islwyn Davies:

Aboard the SS *Peterton* on a voyage from Hull to Buenos Aires, seventeen days out from England, making about 9 knots in calm sea, day bright and sunny. Took over watch at 8.00 a.m. from second radio officer, was relieved for breakfast at 8.30, and resumed watch at 9.00 a.m. At 9.30, terrific explosion amidships followed by another two within thirty seconds of each other; knew these to be three torpedoes, and ship took list to port immediately and began to sink. Sent out the necessary distress signals giving ship's position four times and then found wireless room door jammed due to force of explosion and could not get out that way. Crawled through the communicating window into the living cabin, grabbed life jacket, and ran out on to lower bridge. Noticed there were no lifeboats on the davits, and realised that the ship had been abandoned. Hurried up to the navigating bridge to ascertain what direction boats had taken. Saw lifeboat full of men pulling away astern, so ran down to main deck and along aft and got up onto the poop. Noticed port rails of ship now under water and likely to roll over any second, so jumped over stern and swam out for the lifeboat. Suction from the ship making progress difficult and eventually when not very far from reaching boat was exhausted, but two men swam out with a line and we were hauled aboard to safety. On looking round, found ship had disappeared and only wreckage floating about. The port lifeboat had been blown to pieces by explosions and the starboard bridge boat was floating upside down. The port bridge boat, luckily, had floated off; this was retrieved and eleven men with the chief officer in charge were transferred into it. A raft was floating nearby, so the fresh water tank and stores were taken off. We are twenty-three men in this boat with the captain in charge.

Submarine has now surfaced and is coming towards us; it is seen to be Italian. The conning tower and deck are crowded with men. We know the usual procedure is to take the captain and chief engineers prisoners so suggest to them we say they were lost with the ship. Captain does not agree with this plan and explains that someone else would be taken in his place, which would not be right, but is anxious to save the chief, if possible. We remonstrated with him to no avail, his reply being: 'I was captain of her when she was afloat, and I am still her captain. If you tell them that I went down with the ship and they find that I am in the boat, they might turn the guns on us, and that would be the end of us all, so for the safety of my crew I shall go aboard if asked for.'

By now, the submarine is close to us, and commander gives orders to come alongside. He wants to know the name of our ship, and asks for the captain and chief engineer. Our captain makes himself known and adds that the chief has gone down with the ship. This is believed and orders are given for him to come aboard. An officer takes him on to the conning tower, where the commander shakes hands and some conversation follows between them. Our captain then informs us that he has been taken prisoner, and has tried to get some extra fresh water; unfortunately, there are no tins available to hold it. He wishes us the best of luck, gives the correct course for the nearest land, which is the Cape Verde islands. We wave our farewells to him as he is quickly taken from view inside – as fine and brave a man as ever sailed the seven seas!! We are given orders to cast off and some of the lads ask if they have any cigarettes to spare. The ship sank in six minutes and so we did not get a chance to bring any with us. However, all they can give us is three boxes of matches, which are of French make. As we pull away from the submarine, the commander tells us to steer a south-easterly course for the islands, a distance of 150 miles, but we know we are at least 250 miles from them from the last sight taken aboard the ship.

The sail is set and the voyage commences. Submarine cruises around wreckage, and then dives. We bring the two boats together and hold a roll call to find that eight men have lost their lives. There is very little wind today, and we are not making any progress. Both boats drop the sea anchors at dusk for the night; perhaps when daylight comes there may be a ship to pick us up, having come in response to our distress signals. We spread out and try to snatch a few hours' sleep; this is not easy considering that we are twenty-two men in an ordinary lifeboat about 24 feet long. We have not used any of our rations today as we all breakfasted well this morning aboard ship. Our stores consist of about 35 gallons of fresh water, biscuits, pemmican, chocolate, and Horlicks milk tablets. We shall not be in the boat for long, and even if we are not picked up, should make the Cape Verde islands in about six days.

18 September – 2nd day: Wind comes up about 4.00 a.m. Had breakfast of two thin biscuits and pemmican spread between them as a sandwich, and a measure of water (about one third of a tumblerful). Got sea anchors aboard and both boats now making headway towards islands. Our sail is continually parting along the seams and has to be resewn. Everybody is quite happy and contented. It is very warm during the day and gets very chilly and cold at nights. Both boats keep within sight of each other all the time. Got together this evening for a while to arrange the course for tonight and decided to steer north-east, changing early morning to a south-easterly course, if possible. Rigged up the wireless aerial after dark and sent out distress signals giving approximate position of the boats. This is the best time to broadcast since a longer range is obtained after sundown. Gave – 'SOS from two lifeboats of survivors from British ship "..........." in approximate position 18-50 North – 29-08 West, any ships near please pick us up.' We have had another two meals today. At noon, we had one biscuit and a ration of water, and two biscuits with pemmican and water at sundown, which falls about 6.30 p.m. Now we spread out as best we can for the night, taking turns at the tiller and lookout. Four officers take over watches at the tiller, and the men one hour each at the lookout; this goes on night and day. I stretch out as best I can on my life jacket and try to get a little sleep after first saying my prayers and asking God to keep me and my shipmates safe, and guide us soon to land. It is very hard and uncomfortable on the seat, and I am lying across some oars, so it is practically impossible to sleep. It is getting very cold and all I have on is a pair of shorts and an open shirt. I wish I had some more clothes: I did have a patrol jacket but I gave it to the young apprentice.

19 September – 3rd day: Dawn breaks clear and bright. We have made quite a good headway during the night, and are all in good spirits. The other boat is out of sight, but later comes into view from astern. We are all hungry and so have the usual breakfast of biscuits and water, together with a few Horlicks tablets. I have a terrible job to chew my biscuits; they are hard and I am so thirsty that my mouth is as dry as a bone, and my lips cracked and swollen. I cannot even chew my Horlicks; the tablets stick to my tongue and there is no saliva. I give them away. The ration of water is a Godsend to me. I think I am the worst in the boat as regards thirst. I swallowed a lot of salt water when I jumped off the ship, and I think this accounts for it.

20 September – 4th day: Bright and sunny, still making progress, the other boat is coming up astern. Sent out distress message on the portable wireless transmitter this morning, and again this evening. During the afternoon, the chief officer's boat catches up and comes alongside. We have a chat with the lads – they are in good spirits and we all crack jokes. Their boat is making a little water and they cannot find the rubber hosepipes to fit on the pump, so we lend them ours in order that the water may be pumped out. We decide to have a race to see which is the faster boat, and we go off 'neck to neck', but our boat lost the wind and we went round in a circle. By the time we had got back on the right tack, the other boat was a good way ahead. After tea, we settle down again for another night.

22 September – 6th day: There is no sign of the other boat this morning, but it might appear later. This is the worst day we have had so far. There is little or no wind and the heat is terrific. The tropical sun is simply sizzling us and we are all thirsty. We get the usual ration of water and I sip mine as slowly as possible and put some on my lips, which are now very painful. I can't eat my biscuit so I put it in my pocket. The biscuit I chewed last night made my mouth dry, and I was thirsty all night and kept dreaming of the well in our field at home, and icy water running out of various taps. I was nearly mad with thirst. I will not attempt to eat my biscuit today, because I may be thirsty all morning, especially with this sun. The sea is as calm as a millpond – like glass, and the sun is reflected in it. We are not making any progress today, and are just drifting. I am so uncomfortably hot in the afternoon that I <u>must</u> do something, so I dangle my feet over the side. The water cools me a little and I do feel a lot fresher. One has to be careful as the sharks are with us most of the time. Sometimes they follow the boat for hours and occasionally break surface. There is one really big fellow who visits us every day and swims alongside the boat just under the surface of the water. I shudder when I watch him. A light breeze comes up about tea-time and we are now making slight headway. The sun goes down in a blaze of red and it is soon dark. I had hoped that a ship would have picked us up by now, but we haven't far to go to land, so I must be patient.

25 September – 9th day: Terrific thunderstorm during night with forked lightning, wind of gale force and heavy seas. Dropped sail and let go sea anchor. Rain comes down in torrents and we are able to catch plenty of it in the canvas boat cover, which has been spread out. We drink as much as we like, and I take off my shirt and shorts, and stand naked in the torrential rain and have a nice refreshing bath. Most of the other lads do the same. We get rid of the salt on our bodies. It is cold, and when I put on my clothes again, which are soaking wet, I shiver until my teeth chatter. I look forward to the sun coming out to dry and warm me, as I am freezing cold. My lips are OK now and the coating which was over them has come off. Last night I prayed for rain; God answered my prayers. We have saved a few gallons to replenish our stock. About 10.00 a.m., the lookout reports that he can see a ship's mast on the horizon, so we alter course towards it. There is no wind but we gradually creep up and towards afternoon make it out to be a small boat; she has no sail up. We think it might be a fishing boat from the islands, so put out our oars and we take turns at rowing so that we can catch up with it. There are two men at each oar. When we get nearer we find that it is an empty ship's lifeboat, and as we come alongside recognise it to be the chief officer's boat. The sail has been neatly furled and there are two or three life jackets left. We assume that they must have been picked up by the ship that had passed and which failed to see us last night. We think what lucky fellows they are and can imagine them comfortably aboard ship having a nice tea while we are still adrift. I wish I had been in that boat instead of this one! There are about 8 gallons of water, some biscuits, Horlicks and pemmican left in the boat so we take them aboard, also the sail, compass, and anything that might come in useful.

26 September – 10th day: Dawn breaks clear with scattered clouds, had little wind during night, but it is now freshening, and we are making progress at about 1 knot. We cannot be very far from the islands and should sight one of them soon. Afternoon is very hot but we are gradually getting used to it and can bear the heat better. After tea tonight and in the cool of the evening we have a sing-song. Songs old and new are sung and our worries are forgotten. A competition is held to ascertain who knows the greatest number of songs. Each person must sing the first line (in his proper turn as we make a round of the boat), the same song must not be repeated, and only a few seconds are allowed for hesitation. I am among the last to 'throw in the towel' and so uphold the tradition of my country – 'Wales, the Land of Song'.

HMS *Williamette Valley*. (*Zoboko.com*)

Ammunition ship explodes. Taken by nearby destroyer.

HMS *Jervis Bay*, from a painting by C.E. Turner.

Gun crew of SS *Clan Murdoch*, 1940. (*Collection of Captain L.W. Gibbins*)

Admiral Scheer, showing its six 11-inch mounted guns. (*US Naval Historical Center*)

The *Duchess*. (*Source unknown*)

Able Seaman Stan Mayes.

Lulworth Hill survivors. (*Source unknown*)

Tanker torpedoed and on fire. (*US Navy*)

Rescue by French cruiser. (*BBC*)

Rescue in sight. (*Source unknown*)

Life Boat at Sea by Anton Otto Fischer.

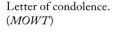

BERKELEY SQUARE HOUSE,
W.1.

2nd August, 1945.

Dear Mrs. Mackenzie,

It is with the deepest regret that I have learned that your son, Mr. George Fingal Mackenzie, who was serving in the Merchant Navy as 3rd Engineer Officer, has been recorded as missing supposed killed or drowned whilst on service with his ship.

By command of His Majesty The King the names of those members of the Merchant Navy who have given their lives in the service of their country are recorded in the Merchant Navy Roll of Honour. I am now adding Mr. Mackenzie's name to the Roll of Honour and, as I do so, wish to express my admiration for the services he rendered and to convey to you and your family my profound sympathy in your sad bereavement.

Your son worthily upheld the noble traditions of the Merchant Navy and I may perhaps hope that the realisation of this fact will help to soften the heavy blow which has fallen upon you.

Yours sincerely,

Leathers

Minister of War Transport.

Mrs. E. Mackenzie.

Merchant Navy POWs, relieved 1945. (*No.5 Army Film Unit*)

'Lord' James Blears.

A Canadian-built replacement, the SS *Fort St James*. (*North Vancouver Museum & Archives*)

29 September – 13th day: Dawn breaks clear and bright, and sea is flat calm, with no wind. We are just drifting southwards with the sail down. Second mate decides this is a good opportunity to overhaul the sail, as we can't make any progress today. It is lowered and some seams that have given way are resewn, downhauls etc. are all overhauled. The chief engineer suggests rigging up another sail using an oar as a mast, and this is done. The oar is lashed to a thwart. By late afternoon, we are in possession of two sails, and now we should be able to make better speed. The sail used is the one taken from the other boat. It has been very hot all day, with no breeze, so progress has been nil.

30 September – 14th day: Wind rises at about 5.00 a.m. and both sails are set immediately. Progress is being made again. The extra sail is very satisfactory, and we are making much better speed. We all crowd as far aft as we possibly can to give the boat a better chance of sailing. A sharp lookout has been kept for the islands, but we have not sighted land yet. Evidently, we have missed them, because surely we have run much more than the distance! There is a small chart aboard, so this is consulted to ascertain the nearest point of land ahead. We find that it is Bathurst on the west coast of Africa, and the distance about 520 miles. We must therefore keep on the same course and make the mainland. It is a long way. Will we ever make it? Still, we shall be getting into the shipping lanes soon, and there will be plenty of shipping, so there is a very good chance of being picked up during the next week. We decide to reduce the rations from today, and from now onwards, it will be one biscuit and water in the morning, and one biscuit and water at night. The noon water ration is cut out. On examination of the stores, we find that we have enough biscuits at two per man per day for another ten days. Horlicks tablets at nine per day for about twenty days, and fresh water for about twenty-one days. This is very heartening. We are OK for stores, and have no worry in that respect, because we will be picked up long before then. The wind died down this evening, and we are only making slight progress now.

4 October – 18th day: Day opens bright and clear, but later becomes cloudy and cool. Wind increasing in force and we are making very good progress. Reckon to be doing a good 2 knots. We are all feeling the strain of being adrift by now and are very hungry. I feel myself getting weaker every day. However, it won't be much longer as we are getting into the shipping lanes and will be picked up soon. I watch the flying fish; there are thousands of them and how I wish some would fly aboard. They would be a treat to eat. We have tried enticing them aboard by night by keeping a light burning, but it has not worked. If only we had a fishing line and bait, we could then catch plenty of fish. We have a Primus stove and paraffin with which we could cook them. Bent nails and pins have been tried, but have proved useless. There are dozens of fish of all sizes around us, and we can see them in the clear water swimming along beside us. The bos'n has tied a jackknife to a piece of wood and is trying to spear the nearest fish, but it does not work. The point is too blunt, or the skin of the fish is too tough. I have a few shots, and actually strike bullseye, but the result is always the same, so there will be no fish for tea today again.

8 October – 22nd day: Wind strengthens about 5.00 a.m., and we are making good progress once more. I consult the log I have been keeping of the estimated average distance covered each day, and in my estimation, we are about 335 miles from land. Wind kept up during the day and we have been making about 2 knots, or more. It will not take us long to reach land at this speed. It is about three weeks since we were torpedoed. I never thought we would be in the boat this long. After the sun has gone down tonight we play a game. Everyone must name three flowers; a few rounds are made of the boat until no one can think of any more. I dream of flowers tonight.

11 October – 25th day: Moderate wind from about 9.00 p.m. last night, which has remained constant. Biscuits finished this morning, each man had half a biscuit each. Horlicks tablets still enough at nine per man for about another ten days. Have 16 gallons of water from tonight. Saw swallow this afternoon, cheered up a lot, guess can't be very far from land. Feeling very sore now and legs nearly too weak to stand up.
Day's run about 35 miles.

13 October – 27th day: Dawn breaks clear with scattered cloud, light breeze and only making about half a knot. Saw swallow again this morning, and later a dragonfly, butterfly, a moth – surely this must be a sign that we are not far off land. Afternoon terribly hot with scorching sun, everybody parched, hungry, fed up and weak. Can't have made much more than 10 miles for day's run. My personal estimation of distance from land now about 180 miles.

18 October – 32nd day: Dull morning, wind has died down considerably. Now only making about half previous speed. Sun comes out and clouds disappear before noon, the sea is calm. We are not making any progress this afternoon, and there is a heavy swell running – just like a ground swell. I hope it is, then we are not far from land. Late afternoon we saw three butterflies flying around. We catch one – it has very pretty wings. How far do they fly from land?

As dusk falls, I think a lot of home. I always do on a Sunday. That little Welsh village in North Pembrokeshire. The evening service is now about to begin in the chapel of which my father is pastor. I close my eyes and dream that I am there in the old family pew with my dear mother and sisters. The singing is wonderful, rendered as only a Welsh choir can. I picture my father in the pulpit, a true servant of God, a voluble preacher of some thirty-eight years' standing – my eyes never leave that pure face full of personality. For the next hour or so I forget my troubles – I am serenely happy. The service is over, we go home, and have a lovely Sunday evening supper together. Father is tired and goes to bed early. I sit by the cosy fire with my mother and sisters and we chat and are happy. I fall asleep, only to wake in a little while to find myself still in an open boat somewhere out on the vast Atlantic Ocean. How often I have nearly given up all hope? But then there is so much to look forward to when I land. I shall be home for Christmas this year, the first for a long time, so I cheer up again. I settle myself as comfortably as possible for the thirty-second night. Oh, God! How much longer?

The wind has died down now to a dead calm, the sails have been lowered and we are rolling lazily in a rather heavy swell. We exchange 'Goodnights' after the lookout watches have been set. Titch reminds me that he has said his prayers, tonight being a special one, and then silence reigns.

My estimation of day's run is 15 miles, therefore distance from land – 85 miles.

20 October – 34th day: Dawn's cloudy with scattered showers and light breeze; a quantity of water is saved. Night brings wind of gale force again with torrential rain, which nearly filled the boat. The pump is manned and we take turns in bailing and pumping it out. Everybody is soaking wet, and lying with feet and legs in about a foot of water.

Horlicks ration was handed out for the last time this morning; each man had eight. This is the last time for us to have anything to eat until we get picked up, so we must from now onwards live on water alone.

When the last of the Horlicks tablets were handed out on 20 October, the future looked very bleak for Johnathan Davies and his fellow survivors. They were, if Davies's estimate was anywhere near correct, within 80 miles of the land, but they were caught in the doldrums, the equatorial belt of scorching days and bitterly cold nights, where their sails hung useless in the calms. Progress towards the land, if any, was barely measureable. 'Boat just rolling in heavy swell and making no progress,' Davies wrote.

While the sudden torrential rains of the doldrums assured the survivors of a regular supply of drinking water, without food they could not expect to last beyond another two weeks at the most. Yet, in spite of the odds being so heavily stacked against them, the morale of this plucky band of men was surprisingly high.

Then, on the morning of 24 October, thirty-eight days after the *Peterton* went down, there was a dramatic change. Johnathan Davies's log continues:

24 October – 38th day: Cloudy, fresh wind, made good progress all day and night. All of us feeling much happier now and the standard of morale is high.

Then, on the 28th, Davies wrote:

Similar weather conditions prevail, scattered showers, and same wind force. Sailed all day and night. It has been terribly cold every night for the past week and we have been shivering all night. This is the worst time we have spent in this boat so far, having been obliged to spend whole nights in soaking wet clothes. I have had very little sleep, it has been too cold and the wind cuts through me like a knife. After all this time, my shirt is now minus sleeves and practically in ribbons. My shorts are not much better. Some of the lads are worse off than I am – one of them, Frank, a young AB, is by now naked and has only a flag wrapped around him. Another lad, George, isn't much better. The cook and Paddy (another AB) have made themselves a shirt each out of canvas and sail twine. Ronnie and Tosh (two gunners) are minus shirts and naked from the waist up, but they have long trousers. The worst off of all is Rotherham, one of the firemen; he is naked except for a pair of short trunks (underwear). When the ship was torpedoed, he was in bed, and didn't have time to put on his clothes. He is very weak now, has to lie down all the time, and does not think he can last out much longer. He tells me that he has a new racing bicycle at home, and for me to tell his mother – if I get through – all about him and that he wants me to have his bike. I refuse to take down his address and tell him not to be such a big baby, and that he will surely get through OK. He shakes his head, but is too weak to argue.

The chief engineer has made a fishing net out of an old flag and pieces of wood. He manages to catch two little fish about 3 inches long. These are shared equally between twenty-two of us.

According to my record of each day's progress we had 85 miles to go before the storm came, so allowing for that, and taking into account the good distance we have covered during the past five days (which has averaged about 25 miles per day), we should be sighting land at any time now. I expect to see the coast tomorrow or next day.

29 October – 43rd day: Same weather conditions prevail, and the wind force remains constant. Have kept sailing all night and day. There is no land in sight. Feel too weak to write much in this diary now. Have had nothing to eat for the past nine days, only a small ration of rainwater to drink twice a day, except when it has been very hot, we have had one at noon as well. Water is getting low now, and there is no sign of rain, so we must only have two rations per day from now until rain falls again, however hot the weather may be. Made good progress today – about 30 miles. It is now six weeks since we were torpedoed.

And so the torture continued. The wind fell away, and the sun blazed down out of a cloudless sky, and the crowded boat wallowed in the troughs of the long Atlantic swell while its occupants grew steadily weaker. Many were now suffering from severe malnutrition and exposure. On 3 November, the forty-eighth day since they abandoned their sinking ship, Johnathan Davies wrote:

Weather remains the same, not making any progress, and still no sight of land. Very weak and hungry, and doubtful whether we can last out very much longer. It is now fourteen days since we had the last of the milk tablets, and twenty-four days since we had our last biscuit. We have about 1½ gallons of water left, and there is no sign of rain.

And then, on the forty-ninth day, when all hope had been abandoned, came deliverance.

4 November 1942: Very hot day, sun blazing down on us from a cloudless sky, and sea calm. Making no progress and drifting south all the time. Lapsing into lengthy silences again, and everybody lying down. Another lad has joined the ones that are ill today, and is delirious. Wally is bathing his forehead with the cool salt water. When this is finished, he leans over the side to refill the tin, but suddenly drops it, and shouts: 'Don't move anybody, there's a ship coming towards us!' I think that he too is delirious, but on looking in the direction to which he is pointing, I find to my great joy that his words are true. Is it actually a real ship, or am I seeing things?

This was no hallucination, no imagining of a tortured mind. Rapidly closing on the drifting lifeboat was His Majesty's armed trawler *Canna*, commanded by Lieutenant W.N. Bishop-Laggett, RNR. Out from Freetown on a routine patrol, HMT *Canna* had come across the *Peterton*'s lifeboat quite by chance.

The final entry in Johnathan Davies's log reads:

We are too excited to row, but it is unnecessary. That little trawler was manoeuvred right alongside our boat, and lines were thrown aboard and made fast.

In a few minutes, we were enjoying a steaming cup of Bovril and a cigarette.

A little later, we sat down to our first real meal for seven weeks – a generous supply of good thick soup.

Did it taste good?

I ask you?

HMT *Canna* landed the twenty-two survivors in Freetown. All were severely emaciated, but in good spirits. Sadly, the youngest, 15-year-old Apprentice Edward Briggs Hyde, died in hospital of bronchial pneumonia and was buried in Freetown's King Tom Cemetery. The *Peterton*'s other lifeboat, containing eighteen survivors, had already been picked up by the British ship *Empire Whimbrel*, which was on passage to Buenos Aires, and were landed in that port on 11 October.

Chapter Ten

The Luck of the Devil

The following is a classic piece of understatement. In his first twelve months at sea, this anonymous young radio officer had run the gauntlet of the Atlantic U-boats no fewer than eight times, been torpedoed twice, had trekked through the jungles of West Africa, and suffered the final indignity of being bombed from a great height. Yet his description of his experiences reads like a pleasant stroll down memory lane. British phlegm, perhaps?

Outward bound aboard m.v. *Strategist* with full crew to join the newly built replacement vessel *Ocean Honour* at Portland, Maine.

There was an interesting list of priorities for the lifeboats and anyone connected with the RAF was top of the list; merchant seamen on passage were bottom! More good news greeted us in Halifax. The *Ocean Honour* would not be completed until May, and we had six carefree weeks at the Merchant Navy Officers' Hostel. Every Wednesday, I played soccer for a MN side, including one unusual fixture against Nova Scotian deaf and dumb, and each weekend we were entertained by two kind Canadian families who lived about 40 miles inland in a small hamlet without electricity, where we carried paraffin lamps up to the bedroom at night. The families were of Scottish origin and called McClave and Nichols, and I will always remember their homespun hospitality. The McClave family ran a small sawmill in winter and farmed in summer. I met Lew Nichols again over forty years later.

After Easter 1942, we said goodbye to our friends and had an enormous breakfast at the ritzy Nova Scotian Hotel, and eventually entrained for the USA, complete with sleeper facilities and a large shiny black man on the footplate.

Portland, Maine, was a most delightful town, clean, spacious and friendly, and proud of its Anglo-Saxon/Celtic ancestry. We stayed in a good hotel for a few days before joining our new and comfortable ship, where general cargo was being loaded, and then sailed north across the Bay of Fundy to join another HX convoy. One day out of Portland in thick fog, we sighted a surfaced U-boat, perhaps charging its batteries, and almost managed to ram her.

The homeward convoy was fast and trouble-free, and I was discharged from the *Ocean Honour* on 11 June 1942, and was entitled to ten days' leave. English high summer – I was happy to have a deckchair in the garden and relax and read a little.

On 21 June 1942, I reported back to the Marconi office in Water Street, Liverpool, and was told to report to the Lamport & Holt Line freighter m.v. *Bruyère*. Heaving my two suitcases off the old overhead railway, I was delighted to see the ship surrounded with crates marked Rio de Janeiro and Montevideo, and the prospect of a voyage to neutral countries and a friendly climate was delightful.

Sure enough, we were bound for the River Plate with a small, but valuable, cargo of Scottish whisky, and within a day or two were at sea. The convoy consisted of about forty ships bound for South Africa, and just four ships for South America, which were to break away abeam of Freetown.

The escort seemed strong and included a crack Polish destroyer or light cruiser with a tremendous turn of speed. For some reason, the *Bruyère* was on continuous W/T watch and, as the No. 3, I was on 8–12 hours watch. One evening I heard signals, which we knew to be U-boat homing signals, meaning that the convoy had at least one submarine on our tail signalling to other U-boats in the West African area to muster an attack.

At this point of the war, the German Admiralty had decided that attacking North Atlantic convoys was becoming too dangerous and had ordered their U-boats into equatorial waters for easier pickings off West Africa and Brazil, and in the Caribbean. The problems of restocking and refuelling were solved by stationing supply ships, or 'milch cow' subs, in remote South Atlantic locations and by the purchase of stores and dockyard facilities in the Canary Islands and Vigo from the Spaniards.

The next night, about abeam of Freetown, the *Bruyère* and three other ships bound for the River Plate left the convoy on separate and independent routes, and we were upset to hear loud and nearby signals from two of the ships, which had been torpedoed and were sinking, one of them being the old Cardiff tramp the *St Usk*.

Anyhow, we kept our fingers crossed, mustered top speed (about 12 knots), hoped for the best and relaxed as each day passed, enjoying the easy swell of the South Atlantic, and one day in August (1942) sailed into the brown muddy waters of the River Plate and tied up alongside in Montevideo to load corned beef.

Montevideo is a delightful little capital city, and it seemed strange to be in a neutral port and see the German sailors from the scuttled *Graf Spee*. Somewhat surprisingly, the third mate included golf clubs in his luggage, and he and I had a round of golf, with a tremendous steak lunch in the clubhouse after nine holes, and finished all square after 18 to our mutual pleasure.

A few days later, we sailed diagonally across the River Plate estuary to Buenos Aires, a bustling, exciting city with a magnificent main street, Via Corrientes, running from the docks to a large monument.

The local English community arranged parties and dances for British crews at the Hurlingham Club and the Church of Scotland. We all spent our wages on presents to bring home, including guitars, and the second mate taught me to play *Ain't She Sweet*. After a happy fortnight in BA we were fully loaded and set sail, well aware that the German naval headquarters would be well informed of our sailing date and estimated speed.

No one was particularly surprised, therefore, when, on 23 September (1942), we were torpedoed amidships, about midway between Brazil and West Africa and spot on the equator, and the three radio officers proceeded with their well-rehearsed routine, i.e. continue to send distress SSS signals for five minutes, screw the transmitter key down, so any direction-finding equipment might locate us, and chuck all the codebooks overboard in a perforated metal box, which duly sank.

Although the ship had listed, all four lifeboats were launched and one was waiting alongside, and we quickly scrambled down a rope ladder in the pitch-black night. One man had been killed, and the other three boats had disappeared into the darkness. Our boat included fourteen of the crew, amongst whom were the captain, second officer, first radio officer and me.

As the *Bruyère* sank, the U-boat (*U-125*) surfaced very close to our lifeboat and the captain and two ratings appeared on the conning tower, holding light machine guns, and I was petrified. In reasonable English, the captain asked for details of our ship and took our captain prisoner. He was called Lawson, and hailed from the small Yorkshire port of Whitby, which has a very long list of its townsmen lost at sea in the Seaman's Church alongside the old abbey.

The U-boat captain, Kapitänleutnant Folkers, of Bremen, had other successes on this particular patrol before returning to his base in France, so Captain Lawson may have survived the war in a POW camp. Captain Folkers was not so fortunate, as his sub was lost with all hands on his next voyage. I was sorry to come across this news forty-six years later, in 1988, as he had been courteous to us, informed us where we had a man (the carpenter swimming at a distance), given us our course for land ENE (and, incidentally – a long way away). We were aware of this last information, as it was standard practice to put our position and course for land in the lifeboats each day at noon.

I felt extremely relieved when the U-boat submerged, but otherwise thoroughly miserable until I tore off part of my shirt to use as a handkerchief and blow the cordite and oil fumes out of my head, and cheered up a few hours later with the first glimmer of dawn.

The second mate, who was at the tiller, was from North Wales. Calm, quiet and competent, he soon had the boat tidy and shipshape and the sail (standing lug and bright orange) erected, and a small jib, which was cared for by our Chinese cook, who either couldn't or didn't speak English.

We were in the doldrums, not a breath of wind, the sea like glass and aware that the currents would not be helpful. We had two water barrels but one had been cracked and was empty. Our food consisted of pemmican, biscuits and Horlicks tablets, and it was obvious water would be our problem. The large sail was some protection from the sun, but there was no cloud, and no sign of a ship or aircraft, with only the flying fish, porpoises and an occasional shark to break the monotony.

I was quite comfortable, being only 19 and fit, and some of the older and fatter men began to suffer after the third day. However, our Welsh second mate, elderly and recalled to sea for wartime, remained cool and authoritative and distributed the small rations to everyone's satisfaction; but thirst was the problem, and we found a quick dip over the side to be a reasonable 'refresher'.

Late on the fourth afternoon, our luck turned for the better. A small cloud, like the hand mentioned in Isiah and the Messiah, appeared in the sky and treated us to a rain shower of about fifteen minutes; it transformed our existence physically and psychologically. The sail was lowered to make a reservoir, our barrels, bucket and various small containers were filled. We celebrated with an hour or two of rowing and organised a reasonable night's sleep with a rota of lookouts. However, the truth was that we were still several hundred miles from land, and not really getting nearer.

Anyhow, on the fifth day, we were saved. A Coastal Command plane, possibly a Lockheed Hudson, appeared in the sky and we fired off all our rockets and held our breath. Then suddenly, absolutely for certain, we had been sighted and the plane dipped down over us, dropped by parachute food, water and first aid, and started to signal.

'What's he saying, Sparks?' I was delighted to inform my mates the message was: 'A HMS corvette has your position and will pick you up in two hours.'

Sure enough, HMS *Petunia* soon emerged over the horizon and we climbed up a rope ladder and were examined by a 'sick bay Tiffy' from Bradford for exposure and the like. The three officers then had a meal in the tiny saloon, and despite advice to the contrary, I ate a hearty meal, drank several cups of coffee, and slept twelve hours in a bunk kindly loaned to me by a sub lieutenant, and woke up next day entirely refreshed, although I didn't recognise myself in the mirror.

A day and a half's sail took us to Freetown, where I was amazed to see a torpedoed merchantman steam in with her cargo of hemp ablaze. We were billeted in a hostel and I was interested to walk around and see a tropical port for the first time. We were kitted out by the Shipwrecked Mariners Association, and shipped home on a troopship in October 1942, with seven days' survivor's leave to add to my normal leave.

Then, on 21 November (1942), I again reported to Marconi's at Water Street, Liverpool, and signed on the Anchor Donaldson freighter m.v. *Moveria*, a smart modern freighter bound for Halifax, NS, and not, thank goodness, to be classed with the vulnerable 'slow convoy' contingent. We made the outward, and homeward, voyages in stormy weather, celebrated Christmas 1942 somewhere south of Iceland, and signed off on 11 January (1943), reporting to Marconi's Cardiff office after docking at Avonmouth.

I booked in with a friendly Welsh landlady and thought Cardiff to be a great city. I went to a huge theatre packed with servicemen (I think it was Henry Hall) and one night to the cinema to see Abbott and Costello.

Then, on 26 January (1943), I was instructed to join the m.v. *Holmbury* in Cardiff Docks, and the first sight of this decrepit tub gave me a considerable shock. She had been captured from the Germans in the First World War, was run by some seedy shipping company, and had a cargo of prize bulls stationed in wooden pens on the deck. They were cared for by an eccentric Welshman, officially classed as a cowman. The senior radio officer was equally appalled at the ship's condition, and sent most of his clothes, luggage and best uniform home, re-joining the ship with no more than an attaché case.

Putting two and two together, we guessed that the bulls might be required 'down Argentina way', and we cheered up a little with the prospect of another South American holiday. Our first port of call should have been Pernambuco Recife, but we were diverted to Buenos Aires, where the bulls staggered ashore in reasonable health. We loaded corned beef slowly in BA, Montevideo, Rio Grande Do Sul, Santos and Rio de Janeiro, having a delightful holiday in the three Brazilian ports. I saw the film *Pygmalion* in English with Portuguese subtitles in Rio, and bought a stalk of about 100 bananas for 3*d* on a country walk, where I also saw a snake slide across the path.

The bananas were duly stowed in the ship's fridge, and I looked forward to carrying them back to Barrowford.

The second and third mates were from Devonshire and were excellent small boat sailors and used to ferry us to and from the shore when we were anchored off in one of the lifeboats.

By April or May (1943) we were fully loaded and set sail for West Africa in excellent weather, and enjoyed the long, lazy days rolling along at about 9 knots, and each evening we had a gramophone on the after deck playing *Goodnight Vienna* and other records.

Unbelievably, we were getting within about 150 miles of Freetown when we received a message to alter course, and the same afternoon our crow's nest lookout reported sighting a periscope. He wasn't the most reliable Taffy in the world, but we started to zigzag and hope for the best. But, sure enough, in broad daylight, we were torpedoed, and the old ship just about disintegrated. The davits holding the lifeboats snapped, and three of our four boats floated away upside down.

By the time the radio officers had completed their jobs, there was just one raft afloat and the ship was sinking. There was some grumbling as we hopped on the raft, but considerable admiration for our two brilliant and experienced sailors (the second and third mates), who had launched the one remaining boat, erected a sail, sailed round to the three capsized boats, righted them and towed them to the two rafts awash and crowded. We then split up into the four boats and formed a little convoy roped together in line.

No doubt the U-boat skipper had watched this nautical performance with admiration, and he kept well clear of our boats and surfaced and put a couple shells into the sinking *Holmbury*, a little practice for his gun's crew.

Not too far from land this time, and on the second day we could smell the dusty foetid smell of West Africa, which was correctly assessed to be Liberia. Our expert sailors reckoned there was too much risk from the surf, and we hove-to offshore and waited for the dawn.

We were very surprised to see, as the light improved, two long native canoes, manned by powerful negroes, paddling out to help us, and they duly rowed us ashore to a primitive native village, winning four lifeboats, which was probably the best thing that had happened to their village for hundreds of years.

I was dressed only in pyjama 'tops', as I had lost my 'bottoms' in the surf wading ashore. The local natives couldn't speak English but made it understood that in exchange for our lifeboats they would provide us with a guide and care for the injured until they could be picked up.

So we set off on the beach, where there were large and unpleasant crabs, and through the jungle, where there were insects and snakes, and we marched for about four hours until we reached a small trading station manned by two Armenians. They had clothes, food, beer and a wireless transmitter and told us we were near to Grand Bassa in Liberia, and after one night's sleep on bare boards they arranged for a flea-ridden coastal native sailing boat to take us to the Liberian capital, Monrovia. Here we were housed with a diplomat who was formerly ambassador to Berlin. However, they provided us with very good chicken and rice every day, and our crew were housed in the local nunnery (Irish).

After a few days, a small naval vessel arrived to ship us up to Freetown, where we transferred to the troopship *Orduna*. We sailed fast convoy with a good escort, which included a small aircraft carrier. I thought the accommodation to be something of a rabbit warren, and slept on deck for safety.

About abeam of Lisbon we were attacked by a German high-altitude bomber, which dropped with amazing accuracy a stick of three bombs. Fortunately, two dropped to port and one about

4 feet to starboard of the *Orduna*, and we sailed on unscathed. We then had a grandstand view of the German plane being shot down by a fighter plane from our aircraft carrier, and one of the German crew floating down by parachute and being rescued by an escort vessel.

Chapter Eleven

A Trial of Strength

Leonardo da Vinci, the fifteenth-century artist and scientist, was a man of exceptional talents, and unusually for one of his kind, also a man of great humility. His last words before he died in 1519 were said to be: 'I have offended God and Mankind because my work did not reach the quality it should have.' For a man who produced, among other things, the *Mona Lisa* and plans for the first helicopter, this was modesty indeed. What Da Vinci would have thought of the works his name would be associated with four centuries after his death will remain a matter for speculation.

Shortly before midnight on 13 March 1943, the 21,516-ton Canadian Pacific liner *Empress of Canada* was 350 miles off the coast of Liberia, sailing unescorted from the Middle East to the United Kingdom. She had on board 1,890 servicemen and crew. It was a black night, and the great ship's frothing wake cut an erratic swathe through the tranquil sea as she zigzagged at full speed around her mean course. Her evasive action was to be of no avail, for on the stroke of midnight, as the watches were changing, a torpedo tore into her engine room, and she came slowly to a halt. The Italian submarine *Leonardo da Vinci*, commanded by Capitano di Corvette Gianfranco Gazzana-Priaroggia, after a fruitless month spent patrolling these warm waters, had at last found a target for her torpedoes. Once the liner was crippled and stopped, it was easy for Priaroggia to finish her off. When she sank, she took 370 men with her. Several survivors who were in the water died of shark bites after rescue.

As the waves closed over the *Empress of Canada*, and she began her slow, spiralling plunge to the bottom, another British merchantman was 1,600 miles to the south-west and following in the doomed liner's invisible wake. The 7,628-ton *Lulworth Hill*, however, was a far cry from the faded opulence of the *Empress of Canada*. Owned by the Counties Ship Management Company of London, and built in 1940 by William Hamilton at Port Glasgow, she was in outward appearance a modern tramp ship but, quite out of character, was capable of a top speed of 14 knots. She carried a crew of forty-one, supplemented by seven DEMS gunners, and was commanded by Captain William McEwan. She mounted the usual 4-inch on her poop, with four Oerlikons, two twin Marlins, two Lewis guns, and an early form of multiple rocket launcher known as a 'Pillar Box' for defence against aircraft. In addition – and this most unusual for a merchant ship – she carried three depth charges stowed at her stern rail. How she was to use these powerful charges without doing herself serious harm was a matter for some argument.

Deep laden with 10,190 tons of raw sugar, 400 tons of rum, and 410 tons of fibre, the *Lulworth Hill* left Cape Town on the morning of 11 March, bound for Freetown, where she would join a convoy for the UK. The weather in the South Atlantic when she sailed was at its autumn best, with the south-east trades blowing light, the skies blue, and the sun warm. There were no warnings of U-boats operating in the area, and steaming at full speed along a route recommended by the Admiralty, Captain McEwan anticipated a trouble-free passage, arriving in Freetown at some time on the 20th.

Twenty-four hours out of Cape Town, the *Lulworth Hill*'s radio officer intercepted a message from an American merchant ship reporting that she had been torpedoed not many miles ahead of the British ship's position. As a precaution, McEwan put his guns' crews and lookouts on full alert, and began zigzagging throughout the daylight hours.

Despite the alarm, the tranquillity of the South Atlantic remained undisturbed, and for the next six days, the *Lulworth Hill* steamed northwards unmolested, but still maintaining her precautionary zigzag. Then, at dusk on the 18th, when she was 500 miles north of St Helena, a keen-eyed lookout spotted the track of a torpedo racing in on the starboard side. There was no time to take avoiding action, but fortunately, the torpedo passed harmlessly astern of the ship.

Captain McEwan hit the bridge at the first shrill call of the alarm bells, and was in time to see a submarine break the surface not more than 250 yards on the starboard bow. In the lengthening shadows of the oncoming night, the long, grey shape, shedding water as it rose from the depths, had the appearance of a frightening sea monster of the legends of old.

McEwan took the only course of action open to him, bringing his ship hard round to port to present her stern to the enemy. The *Lulworth Hill*'s gunners, already closed up on the 4-inch, acted with equal speed, opening fire on the submarine as soon as their gun came to bear. Their aim was accurate, but as the target was so close to the ship, they were unable to depress their gun sufficiently to score a hit. However, the two rounds they fired were to good effect, for the submarine immediately crash-dived. The *Lulworth Hill*, her engine making maximum revolutions, and zigzagging with renewed purpose, made off in a south-easterly direction, seeking the cover of the night. At the same time, her radio officer was tapping out the all-too-familiar 'SSSS', informing all ships that she was under attack by a submarine.

Below the waves, Capitano Priaroggia checked the *Leonardo da Vinci*'s dive, and levelled off at 20 metres. The Italian commander was visibly shaken by the short shrift he had received at the hands of an apparently harmless merchantman. At his side in the control room, the *da Vinci*'s German liaison officer was furious. To him, the simple operation had been an example of Italian bungling at its worst.

The German officer had good reason to be concerned at the loss of an easy target, for at that stage of the war things were going disastrously wrong for the Axis powers. On the Russian Front, twenty-two Wehrmacht divisions, led by Field Marshal Paulus, had only a few weeks earlier been forced to surrender at the gates of Stalingrad. In the Western Desert, Rommel's army was in full flight, while in the Pacific, the Japanese had at last been prised out of Guadalcanal by General MacArthur's men. But perhaps the most bitter pill Germany had to swallow was the determined and successful assault being made on her main industrial cities by RAF Bomber Command. Up to 400 aircraft a night were laying waste to the Ruhr with thousands of tons of high explosives and incendiaries. The Luftwaffe, largely due to its massive commitments in Russia and the Mediterranean, no longer had the resources to mount retaliatory attacks on British cities.

The *Lulworth Hill* had been steaming at full speed for an hour before the *Leonardo da Vinci* caught up with her. By then it was fully dark, with the moon obscured by cloud, and with a fresh south-easterly blowing. Priaroggia, rather unwisely, revealed his presence to the men on the bridge of the merchantman by switching on a small searchlight. Captain McEwan passed the order to his gunners to hold their fire, and being careful to avoid stirring up a tell-tale wash, stealthily altered course until the *Lulworth Hill*'s stern was again to the enemy submarine, and she was moving rapidly away from her. A game of cat and mouse was on.

For another fifteen minutes, Priaroggia's searchlight continued to probe the darkness, searching for his prey, while the *Lulworth Hill* fled to the south-west with her boiler safety valves screwed hard down. Another hour passed, and McEwan, his eyes aching through constantly sweeping the horizon astern with binoculars, began to entertain hopes of a successful getaway. Then, at around 2300 hours, snowflake rockets soared into the sky about 5 miles astern, and turned night into day. Priaroggia had not given up the chase. Fortunately, the *Lulworth Hill* was far enough away to be still in the shadows, and McEwan again restrained his gunners from opening fire.

Midnight came and went, with no thought of watches being changed. Every man of the ship's crew was standing to his action station – as he had been for four hours past. As the new day advanced, and the tension slowly eased, McEwan deemed it safe to send some of his men below to rest, but leaving the guns fully manned and all lookouts at their posts.

At 0345 on the 19th, in the darkest hours before the dawn, when life is said to be at its lowest ebb, the silence of the night was rent by a tremendous explosion, and the *Lulworth Hill* was brought up short, listing heavily to starboard. Capitano Priaroggia had found his mark.

The *Lulworth Hill*'s carpenter, Kenneth Cooke, was one of those asleep in his cabin when the torpedo struck. The force of the explosion blew him out of his bunk and, dazed and shaken, he had just regained his feet when the second torpedo ripped open the ship's side. Cooke, who had taken the precaution of turning in fully clothed, stopped only to snatch up his life jacket, before making for the deck at a run.

Both Priaroggia's torpedoes had hit forward of the bridge, breaking the *Lulworth Hill*'s back. By the time Cooke reached the boat deck, the main deck was awash, and he had only a few seconds to struggle into his life jacket before jumping clear of the sinking ship.

In spite of the buoyancy provided by the life jacket, Cooke found himself drawn down by the suction of the ship as she slid under bow-first. He fought his way back to the surface to find himself looking up at the stern as it lifted high in the air, the propeller still turning lazily. Then, in the grip of the increasing suction, he was dragged under again. When he broke surface for the second time, the *Lulworth Hill* had gone from sight.

It had taken less than two minutes for the ship to sink, and Cooke knew there could have been no time to launch the lifeboats. He gave thanks for the sixth sense that had made him pick up his life jacket before leaving his cabin, but at the same time, despite the warmth of the tropical water, he felt a cold fear creeping over him as he realised that the ship had gone down over 700 miles from the nearest land. Was he alone in this great, empty ocean?

Looking around him in the inky darkness, with the waves slapping spitefully at his face, Cooke tried, unsuccessfully, to visualise in his mind's eye a distance of 700 miles. It was too vast to comprehend, and he turned his racing thoughts to how long his life jacket would keep him afloat. Forty-eight hours, at the most. And then, he remembered the sharks. There was no shortage of them in these waters. He had watched them shadowing the ship for hours – great hammer-headed brutes. He began to panic, and struck out towards the spot where the ship had gone down. There might be something of her left – a hatch board or any piece of wreckage on which to take refuge, anything to get his legs out of the water.

A lesser man than Kenneth Cooke might have gone quietly mad there and then, but Cooke was of that particular breed of Englishman to whom a seemingly hopeless situation presents a challenge. He was also blessed with good luck. Within a few minutes, he had found a cork lifebuoy, a fragile enough support, but it gave him some security. Pushing the lifebuoy before him, he swam on, and was overjoyed when he saw the red glow of a life jacket light bobbing on the waves ahead. Soon, he was drifting side by side with another survivor, this being Able Seaman Hull, one of the *Lulworth Hill*'s DEMS gunners.

With the sea lashing at their faces, and by its sheer persistence threatening to drown them, the two men somehow managed to discuss the awful predicament they were in. Hull confirmed Cooke's assessment that there had been no time to launch boats. Their only real hope, they decided, lay in finding one of the ship's life rafts, which were designed to float off if she sank. They were about to begin their search, when they sighted a small cluster of red lights about 50 yards off. They were not alone, after all.

They were swimming towards the lights when, with a loud hissing of compressed air, the *Leonardo da Vinci* surfaced between them and their goal. A searchlight was switched on, and began slowly to sweep the sea. Accepting that life in a prisoner of war camp was preferable to death by shark bite or drowning, Cooke and Hull swam towards the light.

Cooke's movements were hampered by the lifebuoy, but he was reluctant to abandon it, and consequently, Hull reached the submarine several minutes before him. Two of the crew heaved the gunner on board, and by the time Cooke had found a handhold on the submarine's casing, Hull had been taken below.

While Cooke was trying to recover his breath, he was suddenly blinded by the searchlight, which was turned full on him, and he heard a faceless voice demanding to know the name of his ship. Buffeted against the submarine's hull by the waves and half-drowned, he had no will to answer other than truthfully. His questioner, whom he could now just make out, was leaning over the edge of the conning tower, and appeared to be wearing a naval uniform. He spoke good English, but with a strong German accent, and Cooke naturally assumed the submarine was a German U-boat. His questioner was, in fact, the *Leonardo da Vinci*'s SS liaison officer, temporarily assigned to the submarine with the express purpose of stiffening the Italian crew's resolve, which at that stage of the war was showing signs of crumbling.

The German fired question after question at the unfortunate Cooke, who was at such a disadvantage that he could do no more than answer to the best of his ability. Then the questions suddenly stopped, and the searchlight swung away to resume probing the darkness around them. The beam settled on what looked like a life raft with several men clinging to it, but then suddenly, the light was switched off. The submarine's diesels thundered into life, and she surged forward. Cooke, completely taken by surprise, found himself being dragged through the water. His arm, which was through a hole in the casing, felt as if it were being wrenched off at the shoulder, and his head went underwater. After several agonising moments, which seemed more like an hour in purgatory, he managed to free himself. More dead than alive, he was thrown clear by the accelerating submarine's wake, and came gasping to the surface.

In a blind panic, Cooke swam after the submarine, and caught up with it when it stooped and played its searchlight on an upturned lifeboat on which six men had taken refuge. Not wishing to repeat his earlier experience, he trod water when he was within 25 yards of the enemy and awaited events. From his position low in the water, the submarine appeared to be huge – almost 250 feet long, he estimated. She had a very tall periscope, or mast, a large-calibre gun forward of the conning tower, and a curious square structure aft, which he took to be a seaplane hangar. Cooke had studied photographs of German submarines, and she did not match up with any he had seen. He assumed she must be Italian, although the German accent of the man he took to be her commander puzzled him.

Cautiously, Cooke mover closer, for he now heard that same guttural voice berating the men on the keel of the lifeboat. For some time, the unseen man ranted against the RAF's bombing of German cities, then his voice rose to a scream with the words, 'Now you will drown!' Then, the searchlight was abruptly switched off, the submarine's diesels again rumbled into life, and she slipped away into the darkness. As the throb of her engines died away, and a silence disturbed only by the slap, slap of the waves descended on the sea, the awful reality of his position came back to haunt Kenneth Cooke. He was alone in a dark, hostile world, and his chances of survival were very, very slim.

But, once again, in the face of adversity, Cooke refused to be beaten. Pushing his precious lifebuoy ahead of him, he swam in the direction of the upturned lifeboat, stopping now and again to shout, hoping to attract the attention of other survivors – if any existed.

He received no answer, and soon lost his bearing in the darkness. For another half an hour he swam around in circles, still calling. He was on the point of despair, when he heard a faint answering shout. Nothing was visible, but the voice was real enough, calling out to guide him. Eventually, he found a life raft, whose sole occupant, 21-year-old Able Seaman Colin Armitage, was only too glad to help him on board.

For what remained of the night, Cooke and Armitage paddled their raft in a systematic search of the area, stopping from time to time to listen for voices. In this way, they came upon Chief Officer Basil Scown and, with great difficulty, hauled him on board. Scown, who had been in the water for three hours, had swallowed a great deal of oily water, and was in bad shape.

The sun was well up when they sighted a second raft. It was empty, but much larger than their own, so they paddled towards it and transferred. Their new craft was of much more substantial construction, and its tanks contained 8 gallons of drinking water and a number of tins of pemmican, Horlicks tablets and chocolate. The few provisions from the smaller raft were taken on board, and the rafts were lashed together. With every hour that had passed since the sinking of the *Lulworth Hill*, Kenneth Cooke's luck had improved.

For the next few hours, the four men laboriously paddled their rafts through the wreckage-strewn area, searching for others who might have survived. Their persistence was rewarded when they at last found the upturned lifeboat Cooke had seen in the beam of the submarine's searchlight. The six men astride the keel had been joined by four others, who were floating alongside them on a damaged life raft.

The assorted craft came together, and Chief Officer Scown, although still very weak, took charge of the flotilla. His first action was to try to right the capsized boat, but the fourteen survivors were all so near exhaustion that this proved impossible. Their attempts at righting the boat were not made any easier by the appearance on the scene of a number of sharks, which circled menacingly around them.

It was finally decided to abandon both the lifeboat and the damaged raft, distributing themselves on the two remaining rafts, ten men to the larger, and four to the smaller. They were cramped, but reasonably safe – for the time being. As to their future prospects, no one cared to voice an opinion, but they all had their thoughts.

A final search was made among the wreckage for more survivors and for anything that might be of use to them. The result was disappointing. They netted only a single onion, which was found floating in the oily water. By the time darkness came again, they were forced to conclude that they were all that remained of the *Lulworth Hill*'s crew of forty-six.

The fourteen survivors, six of them boys under 18, settled down for the night, covering themselves with the small canvas sails found in the lockers of the rafts, but sleep proved impossible. The rafts were so crowded, and the sea so rough, that it was all they could do to prevent themselves being washed overboard. Scown was in a bad way, continually retching through the effects of the oil he had swallowed, and Second Engineer Eric Ledger, who had suffered injuries to both feet, was in constant pain. All fourteen were wet, covered in oil, and thoroughly miserable.

After a couple of hours of this torture, the men gave up all thoughts of sleep, and huddled together discussing their chances of survival. Scown, the only navigator, estimated that the *Lulworth Hill* had gone down in a position roughly 700 miles east of the coast of Angola, and 900 miles south of the Gold Coast. In peacetime, the area would have been busy with ships on their way to and from the Cape of Good Hope. Now, with most ships routed well out into the Atlantic to avoid the U-boats, they were truly in the middle of nowhere, and rescue by a passing ship was unlikely. An SSSS message had been sent at the time of the first attack by the *Leonardo da Vinci* on the night of the 18th, but the ship went down so fast when she was torpedoed next morning that no other transmission was made. It might be some days, perhaps weeks, before she was deemed overdue at Freetown and a search set in motion.

The only thing in the survivors' favour was that the weather in that part of the Atlantic is largely fair throughout the year, with light to moderate south-easterly winds and a total absence of gales. On the other hand, rain rarely falls, and the cloudless skies give soaring temperatures during the day, with cold nights to follow. The prevailing south-easterlies would be a help in enabling the rafts to make progress to the north, but the current would be of no help. They were under the influence of the South Equatorial Current, said to be one of the most constant currents known, in that area setting to the west at up to 20 miles a day. The rafts were in great danger of being swept out into the Atlantic.

It is probable that only Basil Scown, an experienced navigator, knew how heavily the odds were weighted against their survival. Had the others been aware, some would most certainly have given up hope there and then. As it was, when Scown put it to them, they were all prepared to make a try for the land to the north. With some difficulty due to the overcrowding, the short masts of the rafts were stepped, and the sails hoisted.

Accurate navigation of the cumbersome rafts, which had no rudders or compasses, was out of the question, and they would have to return to the ways of their early ancestors. At night, the Southern Cross would always be there, shining brilliantly against a backdrop of black velvet, and must be kept astern; during the day, with only the sun circling overhead to guide them, it would be more difficult, but they would manage. As to which way the current was carrying them, they could only guess. When dawn came next day, lookouts were posted to scan the horizon for the help they still hoped might come, and their journey began.

As day after day went by with the horizon remaining empty, morale on the rafts declined rapidly. In daylight, there was no shelter from the burning sun, and at night, no matter how closely they huddled together, the cold bit cruelly into their bones. Fortunately, the rafts were well stocked with the standard lifeboat rations – pemmican, Horlicks malted milk tablets, chocolate and hard biscuits – and the water tanks contained about 30 gallons. At first reckoning, it seemed that they had ample food and water for survival. But as to how long they would be adrift was only pure guesswork. Assuming the wind continued to blow from the south-east, Scown estimated they would make progress towards the land at around 1½ knots, in which case they must be prepared for a voyage of four to five weeks at least – and that did not take into account the doldrums, the area of calm near the equator, which they must enter.

Chief Steward Herbert Thornton was convinced he could not survive longer than thirty days, and he made this known to the others. Basil Scown, though cheerfully shouldering his responsibilities, was seriously ill from the effects of the oil he had swallowed. The condition of Second Engineer Ledger, who was in great pain from his injured feet, was also deteriorating, as was that of one of the young boys injured in the sinking.

Ten days later, they were all still alive, but dreadfully emaciated, listless and covered with saltwater boils. Ledger and the injured boy had both developed gangrene in their wounds, and Scown was noticeably weaker. No one had the faintest idea of how far they had sailed, and the sheer hopelessness of their plight had mentally drained all of them. The only exceptions were Kenneth Cooke and Colin Armitage, who seemed to possess that extra quality that enabled them to keep a tight grip on their minds. As the chief officer's condition grew worse, Cooke found himself gradually taking over his role as leader of the pitiful little band.

On 6 April, when they had been eighteen days on the rafts, Basil Scown lapsed into delirium and died. There were others who outranked the carpenter, but no objections when Cooke assumed command. His greatest responsibility lay in keeping a watchful eye on the food and water. Scown had set the daily ration for each man at 1 ounce of pemmican, one biscuit, four Horlicks tablets, three squares of chocolate, and 6 ounces of water. It was an insufficient, monotonous and unpalatable diet, but Cooke had little choice but to continue with it. The warm waters around them teemed with fish, but without lines and hooks, the survivors had no means of catching them. Cooke fashioned a crude harpoon from a marlin spike and a length of driftwood, but while he was quite successful at spearing fish, most of them slipped off the smooth spike before they could be brought on board. He did, however, manage to land the occasional salty morsel, which was eaten raw, and with great relish.

As would be expected, the survivors' greatest enemy was thirst – and this was not helped by the salty pemmican and the sweet Horlicks tablets. Cooke caught some of the young boys sipping salt water, and took the firmest action he could to stop this dangerous practice. During the daylight hours he was able to exercise strict control, but under the cover of darkness, he could do little.

Nothing could save Herbert Thornton who, as he had predicted, died on the thirtieth day. His passing signalled the beginning of the end, for thereafter death was in daily attendance on the rafts. Some died from the effects of drinking salt water, others were victims of the unrelenting torture meted out by the elements, the merciless sun by day, and the bone-chilling cold of the nights. But in many cases it was the lack of hope that killed. Physical fitness seemed to have little bearing on the sequence in which they died. Each time a man lost faith in ultimate survival, he was doomed.

By 21 April, after thirty-three days adrift, only Kenneth Cooke and Colin Armitage – ironically the original inhabitants of the rafts – remained alive. Both were strong-minded, resourceful individuals, and those characteristics undoubtedly helped them to outlive the others. Caring for the weaker men, a role they had willingly assumed, had also left them with little time to reflect on their own troubles.

When the last pathetic burial had taken place, and Cooke and Armitage found themselves alone on the raft, they resolved that having survived so far they would make every effort to live to see the land again. Their first move was to cut loose the smaller, and now superfluous, raft, which was acting as a drag on the other. Due mainly to Cooke's careful husbandry over the preceding weeks, a good supply of food and water remained – certainly enough to last the two of them for many days to come.

The harvest from the sea also increased. With practice, Cooke had become quite efficient with his makeshift harpoon, and his daily haul was rising. The near-empty raft also was also proving fatally attractive to the flying fish, which flopped aboard, often three or four at a time. These were small, no bigger than sardines, but the two hungry men consumed them with relish, leaving only the heads and wings. Their newfound freedom of movement led to the discovery of a type of mussel growing in profusion just below the waterline on the raft. These shellfish made good eating, part of the flesh containing a tiny sac of fresh water. Experimenting with a rope trailed behind the raft, they found this quickly became covered with the small molluscs. Emboldened by their good fortune, they searched the sea around them for further sources of food, and found strings of edible fish eggs. This warm-water caviar, in particular, was a very welcome addition to their monotonous diet of pemmican and malted milk tablets. As far as food and water were concerned, Cooke and Armitage were now well provided for, but their survival stilled hinged on the resilience of their minds.

As each dawn came and went, and the sea and sky remained stubbornly empty, the two men did their best not to give up hope, but their optimism eventually began to wear thin. They were now allowing themselves an increased basic diet, amounting to 2 ounces of pemmican, eight Horlicks tablets, five squares of chocolate, and 6 ounces of water. Despite this, their physical condition was deteriorating. The presence of a great number of large sharks circling the raft did nothing to ease their tortured minds. Then, on 29 April, the forty-first day of their long voyage, a flock of birds appeared overhead, and they knew they must be at last nearing land. If they could have mustered the strength to dance on their raft, Cooke and Armitage would have done so. As it was, a smile on their cracked lips was all they could muster.

At approximately 1030 hours next morning, the last day of April, two aircraft flew directly over the raft, but at a great height. Cooke set off two flares, which sent clouds of orange smoke billowing over the water, but the planes gave no sign of having seen them, and flew out of sight. Disappointed though they were, the men did not lose heart, for they were confident there would be other planes, perhaps ships. Their optimism was justified when, in the middle of the afternoon, two more aircraft flew over – but again without seeing their flares. They concluded that they must be within the limits of regular patrols from the Gold Coast or Sierra Leone.

The next day was one of bitter disappointment, the sky being empty, except for a few circling sea birds. Twenty-four hours later, on Sunday, 2 May, two high-flying aircraft again flew over, and Cooke set off another smoke flare, which again produced no response. A few hours later, yet another plane was sighted, only this time flying much lower. Cooke and Armitage scrambled to break out their precious supply of red distress flares, which they had been saving for such an opportunity. There was no guarantee that these flares would ignite, as they had been saturated when taken out of their so-called watertight container in the early days on the raft. Each day, the flares had been put in the sun to dry out, and stowed away again when night came. The moment of truth had arrived.

The first flare failed to ignite, but the second erupted in a brilliant red flame and clouds of red smoke, which, lying low on the water, spread over an area of almost 2 square miles. The effect was immediate. The plane first flew past the raft, and then began to circle it, dropping lower with each circuit, its Morse light flashing rapidly. Cooke and Armitage were too weak to make any pretence at reading the message, but they knew that after forty-four days in which they had wandered the face of the ocean unseen, rescue was at last at hand. Tears ran down their salt-caked cheeks, and they hugged each other unashamedly.

The aircraft now swooped low over the raft, and dropped a number of packages into the sea close by. The survivors had no strength left in their arms to paddle across to the packages, but when two drifted close to the raft, they were able to reach them with Cooke's harpoon. When opened, the packages were found to contain a rubber dinghy with a full set of stores, a kite and balloons complete with gas cylinders for inflating, a portable wireless transmitter, distress rockets, and a Very pistol with cartridges. The thing they needed most, fresh water, was not there, but they were so grateful for this first contact with a world they thought they had lost that their thirst was forgotten. Night was now approaching, and anticipating that morning would bring rescue, they lay down to rest, but sleep would not come. They were too excited.

All through the following day, they kept a sharp lookout for ships and aircraft, but nothing came. Exhilaration turned to disappointment, and their sleep that night was again fitful. Next day, 4 May, they decided to set up the portable transmitter. As their hands were stiff and awkward, and the instruction book had been damaged by sea water, this proved to be a long task. The balloons would not inflate, but they persevered, and were able to get the kite into the air with the aerial attached. Neither man had any experience with a transmitter, but this set was designed for such a contingency. It was sufficient for them merely to crank the generator handles and tap out a series of SOSs with the Morse key. They had no means of knowing if the radio was actually transmitting, but throughout that day, despite their weakened condition, they kept the generator going at the required speed, and sent out a steady stream of distress calls.

Next morning, their prayers were answered. A Catalina flying boat appeared, and bombarded the sea around them with dozens of packages. Paddling the heavy raft was completely beyond them, but they succeeded in inflating the rubber dinghy, and in this picked up seven packages and brought them back to the raft. When opened, these were found to contain chocolate, barley sugar, chewing gum, tins of various foods, cigarettes, matches, distress flares, a medical kit and, most welcome of all, tins of drinking water. They also found a scribbled note from the airmen, which read:

Sorry we can't get down to pick you up. Sea is too rough. Have sent signal from overhead for shore fix on you. Your signals are very clear and you have been heard in West Africa and Ascension Island. You are roughly 400 miles south of Liberia but in shipping lanes. Keep your chins up and keep smiling. Keep cracking away on transmitter, especially between hours of 11 am and 2 pm (SOS, SOS and a continuous note). You should be picked up within 36 hours. If any shipping seen on the way back to base, will direct to you.   ʼ

As they finished reading the note, the aircraft made a last run across the raft, dipped its wings, and flew off to the north.

Cooke and Armitage felt that the death sentence that had been hanging over their heads for so long had finally been lifted. Stopping only to slake their thirst with the heaven-sent water, they went back to the transmitter with renewed enthusiasm, resting only when darkness fell.

With the dawn next day they continued to transmit as they had been advised, and at 1430, a large American flying boat came in answer to their calls for help. The sea was still too rough for the pilot to attempt a landing, but more packages were dropped. Unfortunately, they fell some miles from the raft and were wasted. The aircraft then flew away without making any effort to communicate with the survivors.

Four days had passed since they were first sighted from the air, and the horizon still remained stubbornly empty of ships. Cooke and Armitage felt an air of hopelessness creeping over them. But throughout that day they again persevered with their distress signals, which they now knew were being listened to. The night that followed was a bad one, for the sharks came back and spent much of the dark hours trying to overturn the raft.

It was a frightening experience, and by daybreak on the 7th, the two men were completely exhausted by lack of sleep and fear. Their despair deepened into near panic when the handles of the radio's generator seized up, and they were no longer able to transmit. It was as though an invisible umbilical cord connecting them with the outside world had suddenly been cut. Then, shortly before noon, as they were debating whether to risk opening up the transmitter to free the handles, Armitage glanced seaward and, to his amazement, saw the masts and funnel of a ship on the horizon.

Not daring to speak in case the ship turned out to be a product of their tortured minds, both men reached for the hand-held distress rockets they had received from the air five days earlier. These proved to be spectacular, each rocket sending three balls of brilliant red fire skywards. The first one, fired by Armitage, resulted in a badly burned hand, and thereafter the men protected their hands with strips of wet canvas. Six rockets were launched, one after the other.

In spite of this impressive firework display, the ship did not alter course. In desperation, Cooke snatched up the Very pistol and sent up flare after flare. Coincidentally, probably, this had an immediate effect. A naval ship came steaming over the horizon, and headed straight for the raft. Determined that this time they would not go unnoticed, the survivors continued to fire rockets and flares until the warship was within a hundred yards of them. Half an hour later, the emaciated Cooke and Armitage were gently lifted aboard the destroyer HMS *Rapid*.

When they were rescued, on 7 May, Cooke and Armitage had been a little short of fifty days on their raft, and had ended up 430 miles off the coast of Liberia, having covered a distance of 1,065 miles in a north-westerly direction. Much of their progress had been due to the current, but it was the effect of the south-easterly wind acting on their tiny sail that had given them sufficient northing to edge the raft in towards the land, and within range of the air patrols. Without the benefit of that scrap of canvas they would have drifted into mid-Atlantic, there to meet a lonely end somewhere between the islands of Ascension and St Helena, where only the wheeling albatross and the patiently circling shark hold sway.

Cooke and Armitage were very near to death when they were picked up by the Royal Navy. Both men had lost almost 40 pounds in weight, and their hearts were so weak that the blood had all but ceased to circulate in their veins. For three weeks, they were unable to walk unaided but, under the care of *Rapid*'s doctor, and later in a Freetown hospital, they were eventually returned to full health. For their bravery and fortitude in the face of such terrible adversity, Kenneth Cooke and Colin Armitage were each awarded the George Medal. Armitage died in 1950, aged 27, a belated victim of that long voyage into the Gulf of Guinea.

As for the *Leonardo da Vinci*, she was to do little more damage to the Allied cause, sinking only one more ship before being caught by the British destroyers *Active* and *Ness* off the Azores, and sent to the bottom on 23 May 1943. Ironically, it was on that very day that Cooke and Armitage were landed in Freetown by HMS *Rapid*.

Chapter Twelve

The Replacement

On 7 May 1943, a small Indian dhow, her varnished hull peeling through long exposure to sun and salt water, rounded Cape Paman and glided into Mikindani Bay, a hook-shaped indent in Africa's east coast. When the dhow was brought up to her anchor she was forty-seven days out from India's Malabar Coast, having sailed almost 3,000 miles using the dying winds of the north-east monsoon. Amongst the ten men on her deck was one, who although tanned a deep brown by the tropical sun, stood out against the others. He was unmistakeably European.

Seven weeks earlier, on 18 March, the 7,132-ton British merchantman *Fort Mumford* had sailed from Colombo, bound for Aden, 2,100 miles to the west. She was carrying a cargo of military stores, including boxed fighter aircraft and infantry landing craft, which had already crossed two oceans.

Owned by the Ministry of War Transport and managed by Reardon Smith of Cardiff, the *Fort Mumford* was a wartime replacement ship built in Canada in 1942. She carried a crew of fifty-three, which included five gunners of the Maritime Anti-Aircraft Regiment and one Merchant Navy gunner. Like all her sister ships in the Fort class, she was a strictly functional, mass-produced ship with an all-welded hull, a standard triple-expansion steam engine of 505 horsepower, woefully underpowered for her size, and cramped accommodation lacking any of the niceties found in a company-built ship. But for Captain John Henry Reardon Smith, she was a considerable improvement on his previous command, which had been built in the year the mighty *Titanic* made her first and last voyage.

John Henry Reardon Smith, who was a nephew of the founder of the company, had taken his share of knocks in the war, and had suffered great personal tragedy, losing his youngest son, Philip, an apprentice in the *Victoria City*, sunk off Bloody Foreland in December 1940. Less than eighteen months later, Reardon Smith himself had narrowly escaped death when his command, the *Botavon*, had been torpedoed and sunk by a German aircraft off Murmansk, with the loss of twenty-one lives.

The *Fort Mumford*'s voyage, her first, had begun in Montreal on 5 January, when she was accepted from the builders by Captain Reardon Smith and his crew. A 7,000-mile ballast passage to Vancouver via the Panama Canal had followed, during which the ship was moulded into the Reardon Smith routine. Her working life commenced in Vancouver, where she loaded a part cargo in the depths of the British Columbian winter. Hardly a man aboard her was sorry when she finally closed her hatches and set off on the long leg across the Pacific to Lyttelton in the South Island of New Zealand.

In New Zealand, they found an island paradise a million light years removed from the war. The South Pacific summer, the magnificent scenery and, above all, the overwhelming hospitality of the people of the island had for Reardon Smith and his men made the visit as memorable as any experienced by the seamen of Captain Cook's day. For some, the temptation proved too much. Worn down by the stress of seagoing in wartime, perhaps, and dazzled by the contrast these beautiful islands presented to a drab, austere Britain, four of the *Fort Mumford*'s crew deserted in Lyttelton. And who could blame them?

The month-long passage around the underbelly of Australia and across the Indian Ocean, then lying blue and quiescent under the monsoon, was for Reardon Smith and many of the older men aboard reminiscent of those days of peace when their only adversary had been the sea itself. A few hours in Colombo taking on bunkers and then, on the morning of 18 March, the *Fort Mumford* turned her bows westward.

When he took his ship out through the breakwaters of Colombo harbour, Captain Reardon Smith looked forward with confidence to at least another week of trouble-free steaming. He had been advised by the Royal Navy in Colombo that any enemy submarines at large in the Arabian Sea would most likely be lying off Cape Guardafui in the eastern approaches to the Gulf of Aden, a focal point for Allied shipping. And there was time enough to worry about them.

With her dark outline betrayed only by the phosphorescence of her bow wave, the *Fort Mumford* slipped past Cape Comorin, the southernmost point of India, on the night of the 19th, and came around onto a west-north-westerly course. She was bound through the Nine Degree Channel, the wide gap between the Laccadive and Maldive islands, which straddle the way to the east like a broken string of pearls. To the west of the islands lay the Arabian Sea, once a bloody battleground of pirates and East Indiamen, now host only to the leisurely dhow and scurrying grey-painted merchant ships.

Sunset on the 20th saw the *Fort Mumford* some 90 miles due west of Suheli Par, the southernmost islet of the Laccadives. She was steaming at 9 knots through a flat calm sea with not a breath of wind, other than that she was making, to flush out the stifling heat of the day from her accommodation. With the coming of dusk, hazy conditions closed in, restricting visibility, but hardly enough to worry the officer on watch on the bridge. Very little traffic was expected in the area.

An hour later, below decks, Seaman Gunner Horace Bailey lay on top of his bunk in the cabin he shared with two army gunners. The small room was uncomfortably hot and Bailey heaved a sigh of relief when the other men gathered up their gear and made for the door. It was a few minutes before eight, and time to change the watch.

For Toshiaki Fukumura, commanding the Japanese submarine *I-27*, the patrol so far had been a complete failure. Day after day of scouring the Arabian Sea, on the surface at night and submerged in daylight, had revealed nothing more than the occasional native dhow scurrying under full sail. Disappointment and frustration were eating away at his normal complacency, but most of all he feared the loss of face he would suffer if he returned to Japan with his torpedoes unused. Then, shortly before 2000 hours on 29 March, Fukumura's luck changed. Out of the darkness ahead a large merchant ship loomed, loaded to her marks and with her decks piled high with cargo.

Fukumura's torpedo ran true, striking the *Fort Mumford* squarely amidships as the last tones of eight bells rang out from the bridge. Simultaneous with the deafening explosion that followed, Horace Bailey glimpsed a vivid flash through the porthole near his head. Before he had time to collect his scattered wits, the ship gave a violent lurch to port, throwing him out of his bunk. Still dazed, he got to his feet and scrambled for the door of the cabin. No alarm bells had sounded, but it was plainly obvious that the *Fort Mumford* had been torpedoed, and most probably in her engine room.

Bailey fought his way out of the gunners' accommodation through an escape hatch that was partially blocked by a jumble of planks and baulks of timber that had once secured the crated aircraft on deck. As he threw aside the wreckage and gained the deck, the ship gave another violent lurch. He was knocked off his feet and rolled across the deck towards the scuppers, crying out with pain as jagged metal cut into his bare feet and legs.

Fighting back rising panic, Bailey regained his feet and looked around him. He was alone on the after deck, surrounded by crumpled aircraft fuselages and smashed timbers. The ship was listing heavily to port, and appeared to be settling rapidly in the water. His path to the boat deck, where he hoped others were already lowering the lifeboats, was completely blocked by debris. Painfully, he clawed his way back aft, planning to launch the life raft stowed on the port side of the after mast-house. The raft was no longer there, blown clean away by the blast of the exploding torpedo.

Sick with disappointment and wracked by indecision, Bailey stood at the bulwark rail and gazed down into the sea, now only a few feet from the deck. Then the awful realisation dawned on him that in his struggle to get clear of the accommodation he had left his life jacket behind. But there was no going back. The list was increasing, and the sea below coming nearer with every passing second. Bailey climbed onto the bulwark rail and prepared to jump. At that precise moment, the *Fort Mumford* gave her dying lurch and began to roll over. The gunner lost his grip and fell outwards.

Although the sea temperature was in the lower eighties, to Bailey the water had the chill of death about it as it closed over him and he sank deep. He was aware of the pieces of wreckage swirling around him and brushing against his body. The broken ship was coming down on top of him and he was certain the time had come for Horace Bailey to die. He let his body go limp, but the instinctive will to survive would not allow him to empty his lungs and finish it quickly.

When his lungs were on the point of bursting, Bailey suddenly found himself free of the wreckage and shooting upwards. He surfaced near a large object that had the size and appearance of one of the life rafts the *Fort Mumford* carried. Kicking out, he swam towards the object and dragged himself aboard, finding himself on a flat hull section of one of the landing craft once part of the ship's deck cargo. The craft would never see the beaches of Sicily, where it had been destined to come ashore, but it might well save the life of Seaman Gunner Bailey.

Bailey's first move having reached a place of refuge was to look around for other survivors. Balancing himself on his makeshift life raft, he searched the horizon, straining his eyes to pierce the hazy darkness. The *Fort Mumford* had carried a total crew of fifty-three, and although she had gone down in a few minutes, it was inconceivable to Bailey that he could be the only survivor. Yet he could see no movement on the water, no comforting red glow of life jacket lights to show he was not alone – and, worst of all, no voices. All around him there was only darkness and ominous silence. His shoulders slumped and he sank to his knees.

After some ten minutes reflecting on the enormity of his predicament, Bailey heard a faint shout and his spirits soared. Straightening up, he cupped his hands and shouted back across the water, but there was no reply. He continued calling until he was hoarse, pleading with whomever it was to answer. But there was only silence. Then he saw what appeared to be a small fire floating on the water in the direction from which he had first heard the shout, and he began calling again, certain he had seen a life jacket light. Then the comforting glow was gone, and the lonely darkness closed in around him and he was without hope.

What Horace Bailey had heard and seen can only be guessed at, but the voice was almost certainly Japanese, and the glow on the water the flash of *I-27*'s exhaust as she motored away from the scene of her night's work.

To Bailey, it seemed that his life had sunk to its lowest ebb. The sinking of his ship – his home for more than three months – was a cruel enough blow. If others had survived with him, and it was now plain that none had, he could have drawn comfort from their presence and with it, hope. But to suffer in this empty ocean alone, to drift for days, perhaps weeks, with only the cold oblivion of death to look forward to, was a prospect that filled him with dread.

While he was preoccupied with the hopelessness of his predicament, Bailey noticed he had blood on his hands. Then he felt the pain and he remembered he had fallen when the *Fort Mumford* was in her death throes. Feeling with tentative fingers, he discovered deep lacerations on his legs and feet, presumably caused by nails or jagged metal in the wreckage of the deck cargo. One cut on his foot went almost to the bone, and he was bleeding profusely.

A lesser man might have been tempted to lie down and await the mercy of death, but Bailey, having come to terms with his plight, had ideas to the contrary. He cleaned his wounds as best he could with salt water and stopped the bleeding from the deep cut in his foot by plugging it with algae-like scum from the surface of the sea. From then on, he knew his life depended on his will to live and the mercy of God, who had deemed that he alone, Horace Bailey, should survive the sinking of the *Fort Mumford.*

For the next five days, Bailey drifted, clinging to the waterlogged side of the landing craft, his legs and back immersed in water for much of the time. He had no food, no water, no equipment other than a small canvas ammunition box cover and a short length of timber he had rescued from the sea as they floated by. There was hardly a breath of wind, and during the day the sun beat down on his half-naked body, burning his skin to a dark mahogany. Oddly enough, he felt no hunger, but he suffered agonies from thirst. Shoals of small fish swam around him and nuzzled at the edges of his raft, and he made desperate efforts to catch one, hoping that its raw flesh might help to assuage his terrible thirst. Eventually his strenuous efforts were rewarded when he managed to scoop one up and scrambled it aboard. But by this time he was so weak that he was unable to kill the poor struggling creature, and he returned it to the sea.

As the days went by, Bailey became feverish, but it was his injured leg that caused him most concern, as it appeared to him to be growing thinner, almost withering before his eyes. Yet it was probably this preoccupation with the leg that kept him sane.

The turning point came on the fourth day, when an isolated shower of rain swept across the raft and he was able to quench his thirst for the first time by licking the rain drops as they ran down his body. His spirits began to rise again.

On the fifth day, he saw a white bird swooping low over the sea in the distance. For several minutes he watched, spellbound, marvelling at the bird's ability to skim over the waves. Then, as it breasted the horizon, the bird became a white sail, and below that sail, he saw the hull of a small craft. His hands trembling with excitement, Bailey snatched up the pieces of flotsam he had providentially collected. Working quickly, he tied the scrap of canvas to the broken plank and waved it frantically above his head. Very soon, he found himself being handed gently over the bulwarks of a small dhow.

When his thirst had been slaked by a cup of water, Bailey was given a concoction of eucalyptus oil and water, which seemed to act as a stimulant to his tired brain. His rescuers informed him that he was aboard an Indian trading dhow bound from the Malabar Coast to Mikindani on the east coast of Africa.

The dhow was of about 47 tons' displacement and carried a crew of nine, who treated the castaway with extreme kindness. On seeing the state of his injured foot, which had turned quite black, the sturdy brown men held him down while the wound was scrubbed with boiling water. The agony Bailey went through during this purging was excruciating, but there can be no doubt that the Indian rough-and-ready antiseptic saved the foot. Thereafter, the wound began to heal cleanly.

Running before the prevailing north-easterly wind, which was light but steady, the dhow reached Mikindani on 7 May, some forty-three days after Bailey had been rescued. He walked ashore with only a slight limp to betray the terrible ordeal he had lived through. As to the Indian seamen who saved his life, the only clue Horace Bailey had to their identity was the number of their dhow, 443.

The mystery of the disappearance of Captain John Henry Reardon Smith and the other fifty-one members of the crew of the *Fort Mumford* will probably never be unravelled. The ship was torpedoed at around 2000 hours, when the watch was being changed, and very few men would have been in their bunks. Although she sank quite quickly, it seems, as evidenced by Horace Bailey's actions until he was pitched overboard, there was ample time and opportunity for many more of her crew to get clear before the ship went down. It may be that others survived and, like Bailey, drifted on makeshift rafts for days, before dying of thirst and exposure. Wreckage identified as coming from the *Fort Mumford* was washed up on Cape Comorin, 500 miles to the east of the sinking, but no bodies were ever found.

After disposing of the *Fort Mumford*, Toshiaki Fukumura went from strength to strength, sinking in the following nine months another eight Allied merchantmen, totalling nearly 43,000 tons. His final contribution to the war was to sink the British troopship *Khedive Ismail* near Addu Atoll on 12 February 1944. The British ship, which went down in under two minutes, was carrying 1,947 passengers and crew, including British, American and African troops, along with members of the Women's Services. More than 1,000 lives were lost. Retribution was, however, swift. *I-27* was herself sunk by the British destroyers *Petard* and *Paladin*, which were escorting the trooper.

Chapter Thirteen

Indian Ocean Rendezvous

The Japanese submarine *I-37*, at 357 feet long and displacing 2,631 tons, was armed with six 21-inch torpedo tubes, a 5.5-inch deck gun and two 25mm AA guns. She had a top speed of 23½ knots on the surface and a range of 14,000 miles. She also carried a 'Glen' spotter seaplane. In command was 42-year-old Hajime Nakagawa, experienced, completely ruthless.

In spite of *I-37*'s superior potential, in her short and infamous career she sank only five Allied ships, one of them being the British tanker *British Chivalry*. Pierre Payne, who was chief officer of the tanker at the time, here relates the passage of events:

The *British Chivalry*, an oil tanker of 4,237 net registered tons, carried about 9,500 tons of cargo and belonged to the British Tanker Company, a subsidiary of the Anglo-Persian Oil Company, now the BP, was under the command of Captain Walter Hill of Dublin.

Sailing from Greenock at the beginning of July 1943 after a voyage across the North Atlantic, she was posted to the Middle East with the intention that she would later proceed to the Far Eastern theatre of war. After carrying a cargo from Abadan, in the Persian Gulf, to South Africa, orders were received to load at Abadan for Melbourne, where, after discharge, the ship was overhauled and dry-docked as a matter of routine.

Early in February 1944, the *British Chivalry* left Melbourne in ballast, but carried about 450 tons of bagged grain for her destination, again Abadan. Some passengers, including two ladies, were barred from travelling at the last moment, and later it was felt with great relief that they were not allowed to accompany us.

After an uneventful journey of about fourteen days, the ship was well out into the middle of the Indian Ocean and nearing the equator. The track was almost due north and well off the direct track from Australia to the Gulf.

During the day of 21 February, a radio message purporting to come from the Commander-in-Chief Colombo was received requesting our position. This in itself was not surprising, but Mr C. Kennedy, the chief radio officer, a native of Caithness in Scotland, appeared to have great difficulty in contacting the radio station at Colombo. The transmitter, a spark-gap type, caused enough noise around the ship to keep all hands aware that he was transmitting, a practice normally prohibited during an ocean passage such as we were making. This proceeded to well into the evening, and at 10.00 p.m., I personally went to the radio room to enquire when he was going to cease. We already knew that enemy submarines were in the area, and we later wondered whether the original message had perhaps emanated from one that had possibly obtained our codes and was using them to identify us. Later, possibly early next morning, a message was received ordering us to cease zigzagging, and to proceed on our course as direct as possible.

It was with some misgivings that, as chief officer, when daylight broke on the morning of 22 February 1944, I explained to the quartermaster that orders had been received to cease zigzagging. The sea was calm and visibility was perfect. I came off watch at 8.00 a.m. and handed over to the third officer, Mr John Dahl, who was very concerned at this obviously dangerous procedure of maintaining a straight course.

At breakfast, 8.30 a.m. – a lovely meal of bacon, eggs and chips – an altercation blew up with the captain regarding the incident of the night before and the steering of a straight course. Mr Dickinson, the chief engineer, thoroughly agreed with my own view. The feeling became so strained that I pushed my breakfast aside, not feeling able to eat it. That action was regretted later.

At 9.00 a.m., the boatswain, Mr George Dunsby, came to me with a request that during the morning he should go down the after cofferdam, which separated the cargo-carrying space from the engine room, and use a hose to wash out any last traces of sediment that might be at the bottom. As this compartment had been well washed for going into dry dock at Melbourne, it was felt that there would be no oil and the sediment would not leave any track. After setting the men to work, the operation to wash the cofferdam was commenced. The boatswain tried desperately to get me to allow him to go down to the bottom, but I felt it was too dangerous in view of what had already occurred.

Shortly before 10.30 a.m. I heard a shout. Frantically, I hauled on the lifeline, which had been secured in such a manner that he was only below the deck level, and shouted to him to come out. His body was halfway over the hatch coaming, when a torpedo exploded in the engine room only a few feet away. We were showered in rubbish thrown up. By the time he had disconnected the lifeline, I saw the captain coming along the flying bridge and he called to ask whether I had seen the damage. As I had not, I climbed the ladder to the poop deck, and running aft to the engine room door I saw that the engine room was already full of water. The starboard after lifeboat had been blown away and one of the four deck apprentices, Kenneth Bagshaw, who had been painting the boat, was never seen again. Neither was the cook, Mr J. Sayers, who apparently had rushed from the galley to his room below to collect his gear. Two rafts were being released from the after shrouds as I returned amidships.

As I reached the lower bridge, I noted the radio officers attacking the teak door to the radio room with a fire axe. Apparently, it had jammed in the explosion and the radio equipment was wrecked. The ship was in a position 0° 50' S, 68° 00' E and about 300 miles west of Addu Atoll, where an RAF base was situated, and we felt sure it would have picked up any distress message transmitted.

The two boats amidships were being launched, and my own, on the port side, suffered a nasty gash in the bottom when somebody too hurriedly let go the falls. While repairing the damage, a number of cans of petrol were loaded into the boat, as this was the only one to have a motor. Having lowered the boat to the water, I nipped over to the starboard side to enquire whether the ship was being abandoned, and received permission to do so from Captain Hill from his vantage place in his boat, already some 50 yards away. Our crew then descended and we cast off, proceeding forwards, and rounding the stern met up with the other boat. It was at this point that Mr Mountain, the second officer, shouted to me: 'February again, Mate!' The reason for this was that he had remembered that February was my unlucky month. In February 1940, I had been in the *British Triumph* when it was mined in the North Sea, and in February 1942, I had been in the *British Motorist* when that ship was bombed and sunk at Port Darwin.

A roll call was now taken and six men were found to be missing. They comprised the fourth engineer, chief cook, three firemen and one deck apprentice. Just then, the submarine surfaced, and after a short while commenced shelling the ship. Several shots fell close to us and we wondered whether that was caused by their bracketing, or just merely bad shots. Eventually, it circled the ship and sank it with another torpedo.

Attention was then turned to us in the boats, and very neatly, tracer bullets could be seen coming towards us. We all huddled down rather frightened. These were the Japs we had heard about! Presently, I heard the captain calling from the other boat. He knew that I was quite good at semaphore and he was telling me to ask them what it was they wanted us to do. Frankly, I was at a loss as to how to semaphore in Japanese; should I stand on my head and wiggle my feet? In any case, it didn't look too healthy to expose oneself to this sort of action. However, I stood up and started to wave my arms. Many tracer bullets shot past me, but I couldn't see each four between each tracer, so it didn't look too bad. In all fairness, when I started to send the message 'What do you want us to do?' the shooting ceased. Perhaps they were wondering, 'What sort of idiot is this standing up to be shot at?' Perhaps it took them by surprise, but I got away with it.

All this time the submarine had been drawing closer, and now we could hear them calling 'Kapitan, we want the Kapitan.' So, waving to them, we turned our boat and went over to the captain's boat, in which he was standing up. I asked him if he wished me to go on board myself and tell them a story of him not being there, but Captain Hill said, 'No. I'll go. Give me a tow.' We therefore towed his boat over to the submarine, left it alongside, and backed off to about a hundred yards distant. We saw the captain climb aboard and soon after we saw his boat being rowed towards us. As they drew near, the second officer shouted to us that we were to take them in tow and go off in a westerly direction. We took their painter and set off steering approximately due west. We noticed that the submarine turned to head eastwards.

We had been travelling for about four or five minutes when suddenly, amongst the wreckage, a figure jumped off a raft and commenced swimming towards us. Seeing this, I altered a few degrees and ordered the engine to be stopped, and gave instructions for those at the forward end to haul him in. The man turned out to be the third officer, Mr John Dahl, who later gave me a satisfactory explanation of why he had gone off by himself. His mother, sister and brother lived in Norway, and he feared repercussions on them if he should be taken prisoner.

As he was being pulled up over the bow, Mr Dunsby, the boatswain, sitting near me at the stern, suddenly cried out, 'Look out, the submarine!' Glancing over my shoulder, I saw the submarine spinning like a top, and heading towards us, came up at a good speed. Hurriedly, I told the others, 'If he opens fire, everybody over the side!' We were all wearing life jackets so non-swimmers would not sink. Just as we imagined, as he came up to the other boat he opened fire with both machine guns. In our boat, we went over the side like a school of porpoises. In the other boat, which bore the initial burst, they were not so quick. Indeed, I don't think they had decided to do anything, and consequently, far more people were killed. Coming on towards us, the two machine guns on his deck blazed away again. We saw a man with a camera on a tripod filming the incident.

The time now was about twelve o'clock noon. Drawing ahead, the submarine turned and came at us again and again, raking both boats with both guns as he passed. Cruising backwards and forwards, he made every effort to destroy both boats and men. We played hide and seek with him using the boat as a shelter, dodging around it each time he passed. After about an hour and a half, I realised we were playing a losing battle, if battle it could be called, certainly a one-sided effort, so I decided to pass the word around for the men to gradually clear away from the boats and get as far away as possible from it at the same time, at the same time to play 'dead' in the water. As he passed we would sink as far as our life jackets would allow. We would loll about and keep face down. Actually, my eardrums ached with the crack of bullets flying past my head, so I must have been a very lucky soul. Evidently spotting a cluster of men in the water, it appeared to several of us that the submarine deliberately turned to bring his propellers in amongst them. This was done a number of times and several men must have been killed in this shameful tactic. Things were getting very bad indeed; not from exhaustion but a dreadful feeling that our adversary did not intend to leave many alive. During this episode, one man paddled slowly past me and called 'Hullo! I thought you were dead long ago!' 'No,' I called back, 'still alive and well!' Shortly after, I passed another man who was looking towards me quite cheerfully, smiling in the middle of all this torment. I called to him the same as the other had done to me. 'Thought you were dead long ago!' The words were hardly out of my mouth when he rolled over and I could see there was no back to his head. I saw one man who was still in the captain's boat suddenly jump up and scream for his mother as a hail of bullets mowed him down.

Then, suddenly, all was quiet. The time, registered by the boatswain's watch, was 2.00 p.m., and the submarine had disappeared from view. Perhaps he felt that he had wiped us all out. Certainly, he had used up a lot of ammunition, but remarkable as it may seem, he had only killed one third of the number that survived: thirteen men died in that onslaught and thirty-nine were alive, although one man died later from severe wounds received. It was Able Seaman L. Morris.

Immediately we realised the submarine had departed, the uppermost thought in my mind was survival. We hadn't really a sporting chance before the shooting, but here now it was somewhat desperate, to say the least! My own boat was still afloat, the kapok in the buoyancy tanks doing a splendid job. The other boat sank as we watched. Unfortunately, the third radio officer didn't realise he was letting go a splendid chance of us being picked up. The emergency radio was in that boat, but he was only a very young man, and he could be forgiven after all he had been through for allowing it to go down with the boat. So we concentrated on my own boat, gathering as many together as possible. One man was told to get in the boat and search for the bucket and start bailing, another man was told where to find a bag of plugs and oakum for stopping up the bullet holes, and the rest of us kept diving to plug them. I believe about seventeen were found and filled with something. We worked like beavers, and at long last, after about three hours, it was now 5.00 p.m. and we had what we called a seaworthy boat. True, I doubt whether it would have been passed by a Board of Trade inspector, but there weren't any BOT inspectors there to worry us.

The first job to be done was to call a muster of those surviving. As we did this, Mr C. Cooksley, the chief steward, died of his wounds, and was buried at once. There were thirty-nine men remaining. We then decided on a plan of action. No message had been got away, so there was no good point served in trying to remain where we were. The nearest mainland, Africa, was about 1,200 miles away. Our weather map indicated that we should be just north enough to be inside the drift to the west. Putting ten men on a raft in the charge of the second officer, the others were gathered into the boat. Darkness would soon be upon us, the weather was calm and the sea smooth. Actually, we were in the doldrums, of which one hears so much, but seldom sees. Taking it in turns, we rowed westward all night, towing the raft, but when daylight came it was obvious we should not be able to keep this up for long. It was now 23 February, and during this evening a sad event took place. Able Seaman L. Morris, who had been shot through the head and through the forearm, became very delirious and eventually jumped off the raft, where the nine other men had been trying to look after him. He was the only man to die on our journey.

Our boat, which as mentioned before, had an engine in it, had been thought of as being our saviour, but all attempts at starting the engine now proved fruitless. Having been submerged, it was completely unusable, despite the continued efforts of Mr J. Edwards, the third engineer. After deciding that it would be of no further use, a plan was evolved whereby if we could dismantle it we could utilise the space available and bring the men on the raft into the boat, thus keeping everyone together. I had heard of this before where boats and rafts drifted apart. I was determined that if one was to be saved, all would be saved. Our bag of tools was pretty pitiful, however; the main object was to loosen the holding-down bolts, and these were pretty hefty affairs. By dint of hammering with the screwdriver being used as a chisel, eventually all six were unscrewed. I would imagine the nuts were at least 2 inches in diameter. The next job was to get rid of the engine. Weighing 5cwt, Mr Thornycroft, the maker, would have wrung his hands to see the excited group that let it go and watched it plummet down through the beautifully clear sea.

Getting rid of the engine was a major step forward in our survival. All were now in the boat. True, it was very cramped. I think I am right in saying it was only 28 feet long by about 7 feet wide, possibly less than that. We had three severely injured men Young Taylor, a boy of only 17 years, had a gaping hole in his chest, and later, in hospital, a bullet was extracted from under his armpit. He was thrilled to bits to show me the bullet. The pumpman, an Australian lad, had terrible lacerations to his throat. Indeed, while swimming in the water I had told this man to hold the flesh up to his throat, as the windpipe was exposed. A third man, Sloan, an army gunner, was also terribly injured. The ball and socket joint of his shoulder was exposed through a gaping wound all down his arm. There was a furrow across the front of his head and a hole in the back of his neck. Another, more fortunate than the rest of the wounded, complained of a pain in his rear parts. After a quick examination, I reached for the pliers and deftly withdrew an offending item, a bullet that had lodged near the anus which evidently he received when diving into the water to avoid being hit. The man was as happy as a sand boy, and loudly proclaimed he was the only one in the boat with two holes in his behind – or words to that effect.

Watches were set. A deck officer and an AB on together took the tiller for one-hour spells. Three men were appointed lookouts forward, in charge of the carpenter. The remainder had to sit as best they could in the waist of the boat. Canopies were rigged over the middle section, and the sail hoisted. Oars were placed fore and aft along the middle of the boat, partly to let the men rest their legs on it, and partly to keep the two sides of the boat separated so that in the event of an emergency, one side would not crowd over to the other side. The freeboard was about 10 inches, so too much listing could not be tolerated. We had gathered as many stores from the raft as we could find, and a steady scheme of rationing was compiled. I had calculated on a month's voyage. After that I would have to plan again. For the first fortnight, the rations were as follows:

Breakfast	8.30 a.m.	1 Horlicks tablet, 2½oz water
Dinner	1.00 p.m.	1 Horlicks tablet, 1 chocolate tablet, 2½oz water
Tea	5.30 p.m.	1 biscuit (the size of a Marie tea biscuit)
		⅓oz (2 spoons) pemmican
		2½oz water

During the shooting up of the boats most of the biscuit containers had been pierced and therefore, as the boat filled with water, the biscuits in those cans were soaked in salt water. Later, after it rained, by placing a pile of the biscuits on top of the canopy, a lot of the salt water was taken out of them, and

I used this mush to help out. Using the flat top of the first aid tin, about 9 ins. long by about 4 ins. wide, I mixed this biscuit with half a tin of pemmican and very carefully cut the mixture into thirty-eight very equal parts and spread each part on top of half a biscuit. They were very equal parts when one realises seventy-four other eyes were watching.

Thereafter for twenty-two days, the rations were:

Breakfast	2 Horlicks tablets, 1 spoon (⅙oz) pemmican, 2½ozs water
Dinner	1 Horlicks tablet, 1 spoon pemmican (three or four times a week and always on Sundays, when we made beasts of ourselves), 1 chocolate tablet, 2½oz water
Tea	1 Horlicks tablet, 1 portion of mixed paste on ½ a biscuit, 1 chocolate tablet, 2½oz water

After thirty-six days adrift, rations had to be cut to 1 Horlicks tablet for breakfast, no chocolate for dinner, and no Horlicks tablet for tea. I estimated then that we could last for another twenty-eight days. Advice had been given in survival kits that it was not necessary to restrict the taking of the rations, as if one got into the boat, one had an 80 per cent chance of being picked up. Unfortunately, our chances were by no means as good, and I still feel that these rations were just sufficient to live.

We all became terribly weak. For the first fortnight, we used to go over the side swimming, but a strict rule was that the boat would not turn back for anybody. Strict discipline had to be maintained. In fact, our discipline was so strict that it would probably be frowned on by people ashore. However, we had a fair idea that we were better off than those poor souls in the hands of the enemy. If a man accidentally dropped a tablet into the bilges, he would not receive a tablet for himself. These tablets had to be passed by hand right up the length of the boat, and the men at the bow expected to receive theirs. The sun blazed down upon us and we were thankful for the canopies, even though it was awfully hot under them.

We had no rain for the first six days, which brought us up to 1 March – to Welshmen, St David's Day. As the third engineer came from Carmarthen and I lived in Cardiff, it was decided after breakfast that he and I should stand up in the boat and sing *Mae Hen Wlad Fy Nhadau*, the Welsh national anthem. It was burning with the heat from the sun, but we got to our feet and gave a jolly good rendering, despite our parched throats. When we stood up there was not a cloud in the sky. We had not sat down but a few minutes when the heavens seemed to open, and we were deluged with rain. Everybody was allowed to drink his fill as we caught rainwater in empty tins we had saved, and thereafter, whenever it rained we had what we wanted, and any over was put into the water breakers to conserve our resources. Water from the metal containers gathered from the raft was very bitter; rainwater was rather flat, but the water from the wooden casks, or breakers, tasted like fresh spring water.

Each noon we endeavoured to fix our position, but one day the boatswain's watch stopped, and we had to set it again by the rising sun, as we recorded this event each day. Nerves began to become frayed and arguments broke out. We all talked about food and what we would eat when we were picked up, preferably by an American ship, which would have plenty of food on board. Our swimming over the side ceased when, one day, looking like a great mud bank astern, a tremendous shark followed the boat for a while. We got rid of our unwelcome visitor by putting out oars and rowing discreetly away. We saw a whale blowing and again sheered away from this entertainment. I manufactured a net out of the copper piping that led the fuel to the engine. Constructing a framework, I used a skein of twine to make the mesh. Fish were all around us and lying alongside the boat. When all was ready, I quietly put the net into the water and scooped up three fish. They were delightful eaten raw. They were small fish, but never mind; they were skinned and cut up into thirty-eight equal parts. I think we were all reminded of the story in the bible where Christ fed so many on so little. Porpoises would jump out of the water and spray us continually with their splashing. Clearly, they were enjoying it, but we didn't mind so much because we knew they would keep away the sharks, and porpoises are friendly towards humans. We contemplated what we should do with one if it fell into the boat. I shudder now to think of the damage it would have done.

One night, a squall struck us. With it came a strong wind. We used to lower the sail at night, so that gave us no trouble, but as the waves increased we had to get out the sea anchor and lie to it to keep heading into the weather. As it was, some water was shipped which had to be bailed out. With all this going on, a fight broke out. Being prepared for such an emergency, I grabbed the only torch we had and shone it onto those concerned. It did the trick; everybody stopped in their tracks and there were yells of 'Put out that light!' In a very loud voice I told them I would settle everything in the morning. When daylight broke, all were very subdued, knowing full well that I meant what I said. I waited until about 8.00 a.m., then I held what must indeed have been termed a court martial. Five troublesome ones were each made to come separately to me in the after end. Each was told his faults and each was told the penalty if it happened again. I knew that I had the backing of every other one in the boat, and at least two were told that should they commit the same offence again, it would be 'over the side'.

It was really meant. I don't know how I should have fared had I had to put it into practice. The authorities in the UK would probably have taken stern action against me, but when needs must, the devil drives. There were a lot of other men's lives at stake. By the grace of God, it never had to be put into effect. This took about an hour and I thought it was ended, but one naval rating, who had been an optician in Civvy Street, wished to speak, and he suggested that instead of quarrelling all the time, why not ask for God's help in the form of prayer, and would I as officer in charge please lead the rest in just that. I must confess that this took me rather aback, but not to turn them down I suggested a show of hands of those who wished me to do this. Every man put his hand up, so here I was now with a parson's job on my hands, and as tough a congregation as any parson ever had. I thought it over quickly and said, 'Right! I'll lead you all in prayer each morning before breakfast and when we are picked up (it was never <u>if </u>we are picked up, but <u>when</u> we are picked up) I will lead you all to say the Lord's Prayer after me. I continued to say that it was all very well to pray now, but remember to do the same for the rest of their lives. The Lord's Prayer was said and each day before breakfast, a short prayer was given. Eventually, I said, 'Now we'll have breakfast,' and a great roar of delight went up.

This is an outline of the manner in which we existed. Then, one day, on 29 March, to be precise, during the afternoon, hot and calm, Chippy, the carpenter, was sitting talking to Able Seaman Arthur Light. Chippy was facing aft, and Arthur was facing forwards. Quite casually, Chippy said to Arthur, 'There's a ship over there.' Arthur said, 'Don't be daft, you're seeing things.' Chippy said, 'There's a ship over there, and I'm not daft!' So, Arthur looked over his shoulder and said, 'So there is.' Then lightness dawned on him.

This was the moment I had been waiting for. Immediately, I drew my whistle and blew it as the pandemonium broke out. Fair enough, they all went to their tasks as they had been instructed.

In fact, it would seem as though it was quite a natural thing for a ship to be there. Two got out oars, one each side, and started rowing. Another reached for the smoke floats, the first of which was damp. Another took the hand rockets, and holding one up, allowed it to fire. It was rather a pity that the AB whose job this was failed to count five separate stars, and after the fourth, was looking down the barrel. Knocking it out of his hand, the fifth star shot into the sea. The canopies came down, and also the sail. The canopies, however, still covered most of those in the middle of the boat. It must have been a good ten minutes before I was able to turn and look at the ship. Then my heart fell. I could not recognise this outline, yet something nagged at the back of my mind that I had indeed seen it before – but where?

During our period adrift we had all come up with the same idea that if a Japanese submarine or ship should appear, we would all go over the side and drown rather than be taken on board. I told the men that I did not recognise this ship, and reminded them of what we had agreed. Everybody was still of the same mind. As we rowed closer, standing up near the mast, I shouted, 'What nationality?' Men were standing alongside the rails, and back came the answer, 'British!' When we heard it we nearly all went mad with joy. American ships and their food were forgotten. Here was a British ship to pick us up after all we had endured.

The ship was the *Delane*, one of Lamport and Holt's, halfway on a voyage from Calcutta to Cape Town. It appeared that, somewhere about 3.00 p.m., the second officer on the bridge had spotted what he thought was a periscope (just as I had visualised), and sounding the alarm bells, had rung for emergency full ahead, and with the increased speed, the engines had stopped. They had manned their guns, and indeed, the anti-submarine gun was loaded with a shell. It appeared that they had seen us long before we saw them. The chief officer,

Mr Jones from North Wales, went to the bridge, and having been shipwrecked himself through enemy action, took a pair of glasses, and persuaded the captain that it was not a submarine but a lifeboat. As we climbed up the rope ladder one after the other, the second and third officers on the bridge became somewhat alarmed at the number coming out from under the canopies. It could well have been a decoy, with a boarding party coming to seize the ship. However, it soon became apparent we were not invaders.

We had an Australian seaman, Harry Belcher, a tough fellow, and an excellent seaman. He held back, and when all but us two had climbed the ladder, he said to me, 'Up you go, Mr Mate.' 'No,' I said. 'That is my privilege to be last up.' He tried hard, but in the end he said, 'Well, you know that half bottle of brandy left over from the night we had the storm?' 'Oh yes,' I said. 'Go on, then. Take it!' So Harry laid his hands on the very place it was kept, and withdrawing the cork, put it to his lips and drank the lot. He then scrambled up the ladder like a lark.

Up on deck, the climb had beaten us and we couldn't walk, only crawl. Presently, the boatswain crawled over to me and reminded me of what I had promised I would do on the ship that picked us up. Without more ado, I called out: 'Every man down on his knees and repeat after me!' Then, very sadly and gratefully, we all said the Lord's Prayer. Never could it have been said with more meaning!

We were all treated very well on board the *Delane*, and later I remembered the nagging at the back of my mind when I first saw it. The *Delane* had been next to us in the *British Triumph* on our very first convoy from Freetown to the UK in late 1939.

Ten days later, with a change of orders, the *Delane* landed us at Durban, where we rested until a passage home came our way. Four days after being landed in Durban, I weighed myself.

I was 4 stone, 4 pounds! So we all must have been pretty close to starvation when we were picked up.

While on board the *Delane*, the chief officer had our boat repaired, and having it swung out on a derrick, we used it for ourselves when lifeboat drill was held. It must be remembered that we almost outnumbered their own crew, and we were quite happy to use it for ourselves.

When we landed at Durban the local people were most kind, and we all had a very nice time. Many invited us to their homes for long weekends, and we could not wish for better treatment and kindness shown to us. Our lifeboat had been landed when the *Delane* sailed, and although we did not see it for ourselves, it appears that it was placed on a trailer and towed around to various parts of the country and raised a considerable amount of money for war charity efforts.

Captain Pierre Payne was in his seventies when I interviewed him at Cardiff in 1988. In addition to the above prepared statement, he told me:

I had run over a magnetic mine in the North Sea in February 1940 and was fished out of the water by HMS *Stork*, and ended up spending ten days in hospital at Minster on Sea, near Sheerness. Then, two years later, I was in the *British Motorist* when we were caught in the first raid on Australian territory. They came in at high level at first and dropped three salvoes of twelve bombs, and these shattered the side of the ship. After that they kept coming. I was on the 12-pounder aft by the funnel and over the engine room. Every time they came around, we aimed and fired. This seemed to put them off. Unfortunately, one came out of the sun astern and dropped a bomb that hit the bridge. The captain was thrown onto the deck, and the second radio officer was killed. We had Indian crew and eventually we had to abandon ship. She was on fire amidships and she took another bomb. Eventually, I managed to get a boat away. The chief officer stayed on the ship to look after the captain, who had had a leg blown off. I decided to make for the shore rather than the jetty, which was fortunate. A ship alongside the jetty laden with depth charges blew up. But that was war. But what we didn't like was when they turned their attention to the Australian hospital ship, which was clearly marked – painted white with red crosses. They bombed and machine-gunned her. That was not war – that was sheer murder.

Regarding the *British Chivalry*, he gave me the following information:

As we were coming up towards this position, somebody called us on W/T. We were supposed to keep radio silence, of course. But the message was for the *British Chivalry*, asking her to give her position. Sparks thought it was from the C-in-C Colombo. This was the chief radio officer, a man from Caithness. Captain Hill made up a message in code giving our position and told Sparks to send it. The distance would have been too great for our radio set, but he kept on sending. It was a noisy spark-gap transmitter and you could hear it all over the ship, as his door was open. He went on sending it for hours and we began to get worried. At ten o'clock, we couldn't stand it anymore and the third mate and I went up to the radio room. I said, 'For goodness sake, Sparks, why are you transmitting?' He said, 'Whoever it is calling us is not very good at it. He keeps asking me to repeat and repeat.'

We then went down to see the Old Man. We told him we were not happy about this breaking of radio silence, and for such a long period. I thought it could be a Jap calling us.

He said to me, 'Just because you've had it twice before, it doesn't mean you're going to get it again. I always wear a shamrock around my neck.'

Eventually, he agreed that Sparks should stop transmitting. But he said in the transmission we had received instructions to stop zigzagging. Now, we had strict instructions that when we were sailing independent and when the weather was suitable – it was flat calm then – we were to zigzag throughout the daylight hours. As soon as he said we had to stop, I said to the Old Man, 'Look, we should be zigzagging. You've done the course as well as I have.'

'Oh, well,' he said, 'this is the orders. I think we were just a bit behind schedule – a couple of hundred miles short.'

I said, 'It's laid down in the book that we were not to cease zigzagging by day.'

Then there was an awful row at breakfast next morning when I brought up the subject again. The chief and second engineers agreed with me, and so did everyone else. There was an unholy row between Captain Hill and myself. I told him he was making a terrible mistake. But then, he was captain of the ship, so what could I do? We were steering a straight course then.

I still think it was a Jap sub doing the transmitting, although we've never had proof of it. What I didn't like about it was the fact that we were told to stop zigzagging when it was known that there were subs in the area. We heard of ships being sunk in that particular belt. It further upset me by reason of the fact that the cook had put on a marvellous breakfast that morning – bacon, eggs and chips. I was so upset that I pushed the plate aside and left the table. It's just as well I didn't know that I wasn't going to have another meal for several weeks.

Commenting on Captain Walter Hill, Pierre Payne said:

He was an Irishman and he used to wear a shamrock around his neck. My own personal opinion was that he was as anti-

British as some of them are today. But at the same time he was a very jovial fellow. The point was that he was in command of a British ship, while his country of origin, for which he held a passport, was not at war.

In 1948, Commander Hajime Nakagawa was tried by the War Crimes Tribunal for the murder of twenty members of the crew of the *British Chivalry* and the crews of two other British ships. He was found guilty and sentenced to eight years' hard labour, but was released after six years. It was not until 1978 that it was established that Nakagawa, when in command of *I-177*, had also been responsible for the sinking of the hospital ship *Centaur* in April 1943, with the loss of 288 lives.

On 19 September 1944, Nakawaga's *I-37* was cornered and sunk in the Pacific by the destroyer USS *Conklin*.

Chapter Fourteen

Recollections

Throughout history, it has been an unwritten law of the sea that a mariner must always render help to another in distress, irrespective of his nationality or the circumstances prevailing. In the Second World War, the Allied and German navies, with a few rare exceptions, adhered to this ruling; survivors of ships sunk were treated with due respect and were often helped. For some inexplicable reason, particularly where Allied merchant seamen were involved, the Japanese Imperial Navy earned itself a shameful record, as various eyewitnesses here relate.

In March 1944, the Hain Steamship Company's 7,840-ton *Behar*, barely a year out of Barclay Curle's yard at Glasgow, was on passage from Australia to Bombay with a part cargo of zinc, when she was shelled and sunk by the Japanese cruiser *Tone* off the Cocos Islands.

Letter to J.G. Matthews from Ministry of War Transport, 11 February 1946:

Dear Sir,

I am writing to you in reply to your letter of the 27th January about your brother, Mr D.J. Matthews, Apprentice ex m.v. *Behar*.

The *Behar* left Melbourne on the 29th February, 1944, sailing independently for Bombay, and on 16th March, 1944, another vessel on arrival in Fremantle reported that on 9th March she had intercepted a signal from the *Behar* saying that she was being shelled by a raider. On receipt of this information, a signal was made to the *Behar* asking her to report, but no reply was received. The *Behar* failed to arrive in Bombay, where she was due on 18th March, and the owners were informed by the Admiralty that she was overdue, must be presumed to have been lost, and that the crew might have been taken prisoners of war.

Nothing more was heard of the crew or the vessel until, in January 1945, broadcasts from Tokyo purporting to be made by Captain Symonds, the master of the *Behar*, and Captain Green, who had been travelling in the *Behar* as a passenger, were picked up in North America. Another Tokyo broadcast, said to be on the behalf of the chief radio officer, Mr Walker, was also intercepted about this time.

On the 2nd October, 1945, while on his way home after his liberation, Captain Symonds wrote to his owner's agents in Ceylon and said that the *Behar* had been sunk in an encounter with three Japanese cruisers, and that with the exception of three of the crew who were killed, all the passengers and the remainder of the crew were taken to Batavia and landed there on the 18th March, 1944.

Later in October, the chief officer of the *Behar* reported from Java that he had been liberated together with the chief engineer, seventeen Asiatic ratings and three passengers. He could give no information about others of the crew and passengers, except that they were not in Java. A later report from the chief officer, which conflicts with the master's information, states that only the master, chief officer, chief engineer, chief radio officer, eight passengers, three DEMS ratings and twenty Asiatic ratings were landed in Batavia.

The best available information is that the *Behar* carrried a crew of eighteen white officers, seventeen white DEMS ratings, sixty-seven Asiatic ratings and eight passengers. Of these, the master, chief officer, chief engineer, chief radio officer, three DEMS ratings, seventeen Asiatic ratings and seven passengers are stated to have been liberated. This leaves fourteen white officers, twelve DEMS ratings, forty-five Asiatic ratings and one passenger not yet accounted for (two DEMS ratings and one Asiatic rating were killed at the time of the casualty, and four Asiatic ratings are reported to have died during captivity).

It would appear that those unaccounted for are the members of the crew who were not landed at Batavia from the Japanese cruiser, and the Admiralty have been asked if they can trace from Intelligence records what happened to the cruiser.

The authorities in Southeast Asia have also been informed of the position and asked to make enquiries in an effort to establish if the missing members of the crew are still alive, or to ascertain their fate should they have unhappily lost their lives. Should any further information be received, the next of kin will be notified as early as possible. I must add, however, that the necessary enquiries may unfortunately take a considerable time.

I am most sorry that it is not possible to give you better news, and the minister has asked me to convey to you an expression of his deep sympathy with you in your anxiety.

Yours faithfully,
(signature illegible)

Letter to the editor from Petty Officer Walter Griffiths, DEMS, 25 February 1989:

The m.v. *Behar* was a new ship built on the Clyde by the Barclay Curle yard. You have the registration details, and as far as I can recall, the speed was 15/16 knots. At the time the ship was being completed the war was swinging in favour of the Allies and there was an improved supply of armaments and a build-up of DEMS ratings in the Royal Navy, together with a numerical increase in the Royal Artillery's Maritime Regiment. As a result, merchant ships were getting more and better armaments.

The *Behar* was a good example of the new policy of equipping merchant ships more adequately. The ship was fitted with 4-inch and 3-inch dual-purpose guns, a rocket launcher, Oerlikon guns, Browning machine guns, anti-submarine detector gear etc. The DEMS and Maritime Regiment personnel amounted to fourteen or fifteen men, and a petty officer was in charge of the men and equipment.

On the morning of 9th March 1944, there was a light fog or sea haze and I was in my cabin when a salvo of shells fell close to the ship. There was no prior warning of the presence of the enemy, and from what I learned afterwards, the Japanese cruiser *Tone*, together with two other heavy cruisers – the *Chikuma* and the flagship *Aoba* (the names of the ships were not known at the time, but were obtained from the war trial report) emerged from the mist at close range, challenged the *Behar*, ran up the Japanese ensign, and opened fire. The *Behar* was hit before the guns' crews could close up, and the damage was such that the order to abandon ship was given. While this was happening, I was on the 4-inch gun platform at the stern, and had only a restricted view of what was happening further forward. When I realised that the lifeboats were being released, I went below to my cabin to make sure that the navy documents were disposed of effectively. On my return, the lifeboats had pulled away from the ship and I jumped into the water and swam to a boat. Some of the survivors were in the water at this stage, but all were eventually got into the boats. It is possible that it was at this time that the fatalities occurred – one of whom was Gunner A. Street of the Maritime Regiment, but I do not recall the names of the other two who lost their lives at that stage.

The *Behar* sank fairly quickly, and as soon as she had gone, the *Tone* approached, and with rifles and machine guns trained on the lifeboats, ordered the boats to come alongside. Once aboard the cruiser, we were met with Japanese with rifles at the ready. We were then relieved of all clothing, other than a shirt and shorts. All of us were then trusted up like chickens – hands tied behind our backs, arms pulled up behind the back, and the rope then put around the throat.

After a period on deck, we were then herded into a restricted area between decks, where we had to sit on the deck in close proximity. During this period there was some indiscriminate bamboo baton wielding by the guards. Eventually, we were released from our bonds and moved into another space, which was ill-lit and lacking in ventilation. There was a shortage of drinking water and everyone was suffering from thirst. We were taken on the upper deck once a day for our ablutions, for which we were each given a bowl of water containing about 2 pints. Toilet facilities had been constructed from timber and outrigged over the ship's side.

We were aboard the *Tone* for six days while the squadron presumably completed its patrol, and on 15th March, the three cruisers anchored off Batavia. Fifteen of the Europeans, comprising heads of sections, the captain, chief officer, chief engineer, second engineer, radio officer, myself, two ASDIC ratings, two women passengers and other passengers were then transferred to one of the other cruisers, probably the flagship *Aoba*. From there we were then put ashore and placed in an empty room of a building that was probably the former local office of the KPM shipping company. The next day, seventeen of the Indian crew were put into the room, and it was apparent that they were mostly members of the crew who could speak some English.

After a day or so in this unsatisfactory accommodation, five of the Europeans – the chief officer, chief engineer, two RN ASDIC ratings and myself, together with a Chinese passenger, plus six or seven of the Indians – were taken to a POW camp in Batavia. The two women passengers were taken away separately

(I was able to trace them in the ladies' camp and visited the camp when the war was finished). Our party was kept in isolation from the other POWs for several months, during which time we were subject to interrogation in various buildings in Batavia. After several months in the isolation block, we were eventually transferred to the main camp.

From the time of being segregated from the other members of the party who had put ashore in the first instance, we had no knowledge of their whereabouts or the fate of the balance of the crew we had left aboard the *Tone*.

In the 1950s, I was a shipping master at the Royal Docks in London, and at different times, I met W. Phillips – who was then a captain – and Captain Symonds, who was then doing relief work. I also met some of the Indian crew who had been incarcerated with us. Captain Symonds and his party had been transferred to camps in Japan, where I believe they were put to work in the mines. These chance meetings did not throw any light on what had happened to the remainder of the crew. This was an unsolved mystery until I saw a copy of *The Knights of the Bushido* in the library and to my surprise, here was the answer to the question.

I am not aware that you know the fate of these seventy-two people – but presumably, you know that they were all beheaded.

Statement by Mrs Phillips, widow of Captain William Phillips, interviewed by the editor 8 August 1988:

The Japanese cruiser warned the *Behar* not to send out RRR message, but radio officer tried to get message away. Then the *Tone* opened fire. Four bells were just striking and Phillips was ironing a pair of trousers. He rushed up on deck, then dashed back to switch off the iron. He and the captain stayed behind and each searched one side of the ship to see if anyone was left behind. Then they shook hands and jumped overboard. Others had already been picked up by the *Tone*'s boats. Left in the water were the captain, chief officer, chief engineer, two Dutch women, and the serang, or butler. They managed to hold on to floating wreckage, but were in the water for a long time. Eventually, a boat came back for them.

When taken on board the cruiser the survivors were beaten with baseball bats by the crew. They were shut down below decks and allowed up twice a day and once at night for exercise. At first they thought they were being taken to Japan, but deduced from the stars that this was not so.

On arrival at the camp in Batavia, Phillips, who had complained bitterly about their treatment, was put into solitary confinement. His punishment cell resembled a large dog kennel, with no lights. He was bound hand and foot, with his head in a kind of stock, so that he had to keep his head up or choke. He said that the only thing that kept him sane was the sight of a plant growing seen through a knothole.

The camp was in the middle of a jungle, and when men went mad, as they did, they were pushed out into the jungle and left to wander and starve. The *Behar* survivors lived under these hellish conditions for nearly eighteen months, being forced to clear the jungle with their bare hands. Phillips maintained that only the dropping of the atom bombs on Hiroshima and Nagasaki saved them.

Even when the war ended, it was many months before the *Behar* survivors were sent home. First the America POWs were shipped out, then the Australians, and then the Dutch. It seemed that the British were to be forgotten. Edwina Mountbatten visited the camp and saw their plight. She quickly arranged for a naval vessel to take them to Singapore, from where they were finally repatriated to the UK.

When he emerged from the Japanese POW camp on Batavia, William Phillips, normally short and of ample proportions, had been reduced to mere skin and bones. He eventually returned to sea, but his experiences in captivity never ceased to haunt him. He went on to command ships with the Hain Line, and retired aged 60 in 1966. A year later, he was dead.

At the War Crimes Trial held in Tokyo in 1945 it was revealed that Vice Admiral Sakonju, who commanded the Japanese squadron, had ordered Captain Mayuzumi, commanding the cruiser *Tone*, to take only the minimum number of prisoners from the *Behar*, and to 'dispose of the others'. Mayuzumi, being a Christian, refused to carry out this order, but he was overruled. Mayuzumi told the court:

> On the evening of 18 March I was told by Captain Mii that the execution of the prisoners still remaining on board must be carried out that night at sea. I refused to be associated with the execution so the captain issued orders direct to Lieutenant Ishihara. I cannot now remember the names of the members of the execution party, but I learned that most of them were gunroom officers, although Lieutenant Tani and a few other wardroom officers were in the party. I later heard Sub Lieutenants Tanaka and Otsuka boasting of their participation in the execution. As I was not an eyewitness, I could not describe the actual method used, but I did hear that the prisoners were knocked down by a jab in the stomach and a kick in the testicles, and then beheaded.

Chapter Fifteen

The China Coaster

The *Nancy Moller* was a typical 'China coaster' of the 1940s. Built in Sunderland in 1907, she was a coal-burning steamer of 3,916 tons gross, owned by the Moller Line of London, and registered in Shanghai. She was manned by a crew of sixty-five, which in keeping with her calling was truly cosmopolitan.

In command of the *Nancy Moller* was 31-year-old Britisher Captain James Hansen, who resided in Calcutta, while his second in command was Chief Officer Neil McLeod Russell Morris from Dunfermline. Completing the bridge team were Second Officer Shih Kao Chu and Third Officer Sui Yuang Chui, both originating from Hong Kong. The radio room was manned by First Radio Officer John Goodson, also living in Calcutta, and Second Radio Officer Peter Quinn from Galway.

The *Nancy Moller*'s engine room was under the watchful eye of Russian-born Chief Engineer Danielovitch Tcherovsky, backed up by Second Engineer Hsin Shing, Third Engineer Ah Ching and Fourth Engineer Kong Kwok Shun, who were all Hong Kong based.

The ship's ratings, deck, engine room and catering personnel were all of Indian nationality, and her wartime armament, a 12-pounder and five 20mm Oerlikons, was manned by seven British DEMS gunners.

The *Nancy Moller* sailed from Durban on 28 February 1944 with a full cargo of coal for the Admiralty coaling station at Colombo. Passing to the east of Madagascar to avoid enemy submarines said to be haunting the Mozambique Channel, she was 300 miles south of Ceylon when, on the morning of 18 March, she was torpedoed by the Japanese submarine *I-165,* under the command of Lieutenant T. Shimizu. Second Officer Shih Kao Chu wrote the following description of the incident:

On 28 February 1944, after having adjusted compasses and tested D.G. Range, SS *Nancy Moller* proceeded independently on her way from Durban to Colombo with a load of coal. The crew were wondering why Colombo does not get its coal supply from Calcutta, which lies only one third the distance away.

For the first week, owing to rough weather, the ship was making slow progress, and shipping seawater constantly on the fore and aft decks. On 3 March, we received Admiralty message that one ship was torpedoed in latitude 2.01 N, longitude 76.20 (?) E, which position lay quite close to the track we were instructed to take. On 17 March, the ship passed that position at 22.00 SAT by DR.

Then, at 0015 hours on the 18th, I saw the skipper entering the chartroom with the First Radio Officer. Coming out after fifteen minutes, he told me that the Admiralty message had inserted Position 'J' between 'G' and 'H', and diverted our track to the eastward to avoid, ostensibly, the spot where the last ship was torpedoed; that he had laid the new track on the chart, course to be changed to 90° (true) from one o'clock; and that as the distance to go would have thus increased by 50 miles, he left orders for the First Mate to use zigzag diagram No. 11 from 6.00 a.m. in order to reach Colombo Monday morning. (So far, we used diagram No. 6, which discounted the speed by 14 per cent, while No. 11 only 5 per cent.)

At 2.45 a.m. (same watch), I got ex-meridian latitude by star Alpha Centauri as 2° 14' N, and at 8.25 a.m., the longitude by sun was 78° 23' E. (The position line runs almost N and S.) Third Officer was on lookout on the bridge.

At 8.40 a.m. SAT (or 3.32 GMT), the first torpedo from port side struck the engine room with a great concussion of the ship. I grasped my life jacket and ran out of my room. Then, almost in succession, the second torpedo hit the deep tank under the bridge. As soon as I reached the open deck, the sea was already in level, so I was drawn down to an unknown depth by the suction, and swallowed many mouthfuls of seawater. As I came slowly up again I caught hold of a lifebuoy nearby, on which three other persons were already hanging. Looking around, I could see nothing of the ship but floating woods and ashes. We saw an upturned lifeboat not far away, so we struggled ahead and reached it.

Hardly had we rested, when the submarine surfaced. It was painted greyish-dark, without any identification marks, mounted one 4-inch gun on the foredeck, and had a crew of more than twenty bustling about. She reached one of the rafts, on which were the gunlayer, D.B. Fryers, Second Engineer H.T. Shing, the fitter, and three other Indians. They were ordered to board the sub. Fryers was taken down for examination and the other five were made to kneel down towards the bow. The second engineer was shot twice and kicked into the sea. As he had no life jacket, he was soon drowned. The fitter received one shot, and as he was wearing his life jacket, he managed to struggle in the water, and was finally picked up by us. The other three Indians were merely driven into the water without being shot, so they were all rescued later on. Afterwards, the Japs turned the machine gun towards the other rafts and opened fire.

The survivors were nimble enough to hide their bodies underwater, with hands grasping the becket lines, so nobody was known to be hit. The sub, being satisfied that no life was left, drew away out of sight. Then we started to pick up anyone in the water; those who had life jackets or were on a piece of wood as support were all saved. Thirty-two survivors were counted. We gathered the four rafts together and attempted to get the water and food tanks out of the upturned boat, but in vain.

We settled down on the raft for that day and night. The next day, thinking that no distress could be possibly sent out and that the nearest land was within 200 miles, we determined to strike northwards along the ship's track, expecting to get favourable weather, as the weather chart promised. As we had no compass on any of the rafts, I led the way by observing the general direction of the sun and stars, and told them to follow and keep together. We pulled the second day and night in turns.

Food and water were strictly rationed (four dippers of water, six tablets of chocolate and a quarter piece of biscuit per day, per head).

On the third day (20 March), the weather became worse, and one of the rafts was too far behind to be seen. As there was moderate easterly swell prevailing, we put out the sea anchor for the night and sat on the raft dipping our feet in the seawater, which constantly awashed the raft. The days were scorching hot, and the nights, with frequent rains and freshening winds, made us feel doubly cold. We saw many small fishes swimming about the raft, almost within reach of our arms. We regretted very much that we did not have fishing kits on any of the rafts; otherwise we would have had hearty meals every day.

On the fourth day (21 March), towards evening, about one and a half hours before sunset, we sighted an aircraft far away in the west direction, flying northwards. I at once made a smoke signal (other crew waved the yellow flag), and the other raft nearby also struck a smoke signal to follow suit. But as the atmospheric pressure was low, the smoke clung to the water surface, and so the aircraft did not see the rafts or the smoke at all, but continued its flight northwards and was soon out of sight in the clouds. Anyway, we were full of hope. Colombo must have expected the ship to arrive on the previous day (20 March), and since she did not turn up this day, naturally the aircraft was sent for reconnaissance. If it could not find any trace of the ship, she must be presumed lost, so the next day we would expect more aircraft out to search for survivors. That night all our minds were set at ease, and we were ready to keep a sharp lookout for any rescue ship or aircraft the following day.

On the fifth morning (22 March), when it was only slightly whitish on the horizon, the men on the lookout shouted out: 'Ship, ship!' Indeed, we saw a small black shadow in the northerly direction crawling directly towards us. I snatched up the signalling torch and shot off a series of SOSs, which were received immediately. Then I flashed the message: '*NANCY MOLLER* TORPEDOED FOUR DAYS AGO. FOUR RAFTS NEARBY.' At that moment, the daylight already crept on and we found that the ship was a cruiser. She made several circles around, and picked up all the survivors off the four rafts in succession. By 4.10 GMT, all were safe on board. Four days later (26 March), we were landed at Mauritius.

The following was dictated to an Admiralty representative by Danielovitch Tcherovsky, the *Nancy Moller*'s Russian chief engineer, at Durban on 3 April 1944:

Another heavy explosion occurred under the saloon and I knew we had been hit by a second torpedo in the vicinity of the deep tank and No. 2 hold. I then came out of my room and saw the saloon floor burst upwards and the water was pouring through with terrific force.

I hurried out on deck on the starboard side. The ship was listing heavily to port, and water poured over the deck and hurled me into the water. I estimate the time from the first explosion till the ship sank to be about one minute. I do not know how long I was under the water, but when I came to the surface and looked around, the ship had gone and the sea in the vicinity was covered with wreckage. I caught hold of a lifebuoy that was floating nearby.

I saw the chief officer (Mr Morris) struggling in the water some distance away. I also saw the third officer about 40 feet away, struggling in the water. I saw all four rafts floating on the surface.

Just then, the submarine surfaced about 40 or 50 yards away. A voice from the submarine shouted: 'Captain! Chief Engineer!' I kept swimming away from the submarine. I saw the chief gunner (Mr Fryer), second engineer (Mr Shing), fitter (Mr Wong Chi May) and three lascars on a raft, which was very close to the port side of the submarine. The submarine again shouted for the captain and chief engineer, and somebody from the raft replied: 'Captain dead, chief engineer dead.' The submarine then threw a rope to the raft, pulled it alongside and ordered all the men on the raft onto the forward deck of the submarine. I saw the Japanese officer in the conning tower of the submarine making signs to take the chief gunner (Mr Fryer) down the hatch.

The Chinese second engineer (Mr Shing) and the Chinese fitter (Mr Wong Chi May) were taken onto the after deck. The second engineer was told to go on the starboard side, and the fitter was told to go on the port side. The Japanese in charge of these two men then shot them with a revolver from a very close range, and they fell into the sea, one on each side. The second engineer had no life jacket, but the fitter had. The Japanese who had shot them then went forward to the three lascars who were standing on the deck. He said something to them, and pushed them off the submarine into the water without harming them.

The submarine then circled around the vicinity and by this time there were survivors on all four rafts, and I myself had reached one of the rafts, but was not yet onto it. The submarine then opened fire on the survivors on the rafts with a machine gun, and everybody then jumped into the water. I was clinging to the raft and a bullet struck the raft and slightly wounded me in the right thumb. The submarine then cruised on the surface, on what I think was eastwards, and was visible for about two hours afterwards on the surface.

In the meantime, the survivors had resumed their positions on the rafts, and I picked up the fitter, who had struggled onto a hatch cover, in spite of his bullet wound. The second officer (Mr Chu) was also on my raft, and we contacted the other rafts, telling them to keep all together and head north-east.

Three of the rafts were undamaged and one was damaged. Four European gunners were on this damaged raft. Fortunately, the water tanks were all renewed in Cape Town, and there was ample water for everybody.

I did not see Captain Hansen at any time after 8.25 a.m., when I left his cabin.

At the time of the torpedoing, the fourth engineer was on duty in the engine room.

The chief officer (Mr Morris), the third officer (Mr Yung Chin Sui), and the second engineer (Mr H.T. Shing), who was shot, were lost. Their bodies were later seen floating in the water.

Mr Morris did not have a life jacket on. Mr Shing (second engineer) also had no life jacket on.

On completion of her patrol in the Indian Ocean, *I-165* was sent to the island of Biak, on the north coast of western New Guinea, to assist in troop movements, in the course of which assignment she was heavily depth-charged by three US Navy subchasers and received major damage. She retired to Sasebo for repairs, and thereafter served as a mother ship for mini submarines until June 1945, when she was caught on the surface and sunk by American aircraft.

Chapter Sixteen

Death by the Sword

James Blears, Hawaii, March 1989.

Time sure flies by. The forty-fifth year since the sinking of the *Tjisalak* in the Indian Ocean, 26 March 1944. Through my eyes, here is the account, which is as close as you can get.

Torpedoed about 6.00 a.m., 26 March, 78 degrees east, 3 degrees south. Ship sank in about nine minutes on an even keel. I was second radio officer and had the 12–4 watch. My job (if off duty) was to check the radio cabin to see that the chief radio man was OK and getting off the distress message (SSS). Then to proceed to the after gun deck to get the portable radio and a rifle and ammo into the small boat used by the British Navy gun crew, then to assist in the operation of the 4-inch gun (we took a course on gunnery so we could help out in case of anyone who had been wounded could not be there).

Ship was sinking on an even keel very quickly. We fired several rounds at a periscope which had popped up several hundred yards away. By this time, the lifeboat was practically in the water so I got in and unhooked the boat so it would not be dragged down with the ship.

We then all dived off and climbed into the boat. One of the gunners had struck his head on an empty shell casing, so I dived back in and pulled him to the lifeboat. There were four boats now with a total of 100 persons (three engine room ratings had been killed by the torpedo), thirteen Dutch officers, two Leeringen (apprentices), ten

British Royal Navy gunners, fifty-one Chinese, twenty-two lascars and five European First Class passengers (Australian Commandos, Army going to India for the Burma fighting), and an American Red Cross nurse, female, Mrs Verna Gorden Britain. Her husband was a British Army captain stationed in India, and she was going to meet him on leave. Captain Hen (Dutch master) was in the boat with an engine, with the nurse, Australians, chief radio officer, and several others. Soon, a periscope popped up, then two more (same sub) and the sub surfaced about a hundred yards or so away from us. Someone on the sub hailed and waved, so the captain started his engine and sailed over to the sub. We saw them climb aboard and go into the conning tower. Then the sub crew waved us all to come alongside, which we all did. Our boat was the last boat alongside. Afterwards we found out it was the *I-8*, a large Japanese submarine that carried a small seaplane for scouting.

We climbed aboard and the Japanese took our rings and watches, after which most of us were stripped. The officers had pistols and swords and belted us with the flat of the swords in the direction forward of the conning tower past a deck gun. They then hit us again to squat down on the deck. We were all then sitting with bowed heads (all except the captain and his party, who I told you were taken below earlier). The sub was now underway, maybe doing 5 to 8 knots. One guard was yelling all the time: 'You look back, you shot!' The only one of us who had anything on was a lascar sitting in front of me, and for some reason he was still wearing his life jacket.

They began taking the Dutch officers behind where I was sitting and we heard shots and screams. I thought that I had better jump overboard and take a chance, but just before I had made up my mind, the lascar suddenly dived overboard. He was immediately machine-gunned and was collapsed in the life jacket as we continued on course.

That was out for me. They then began dragging the lascars forward and bending them down with their arms behind them and began chopping off heads with their swords. They were taking moving pictures with a big camera of these events.

I was in a daze. Didn't know what to do, when I was hit with the flat of a sword and led to the twin gun area. There I saw the British Navy gunners all together and tied with their hands behind their backs. One gunner punched one of the guards as he was being tied and they spun him around and hit him full-on with the sword, cutting deep into his head and back, and he just fell overboard.

I was tied to a Dutch deck officer, Peter Bronger, with maybe 4 feet of rope between us, hands behind back. I had kept my hands as wide as I could, and felt I could get one hand free. We were then belted with the flat of the swords and pushed to walk aft alongside the conning tower. I knew there was someone waiting behind the tower. I was in the lead. Two Japanese attacked us, one with a sword and one with a sledgehammer. I ducked the sword, kicked out at the guy with the hammer, and diving overboard, pulling my one hand free, but still tied to the Dutch officer. I hit the water on the starboard side and tried to stay under.

The twin screws of the sub chopped past, and as I hit the surface, bullets were popping around. I dived, trying to pull my friend under the water. Up to the surface again and saw that there were two or three in chairs shooting with rifles, and there were also machine guns firing from the conning tower. After diving under several times, and the sub now moving away, I checked my friend, who was still tied to me (to my one wrist, as I had the other one free). Peter was bleeding badly from the back and mouth and was unconscious. I stayed with him for a while, then let him go and began swimming in the direction where I thought the empty lifeboats were. The swells were a good size, but the sea was smooth. I tried to make out a pattern of clouds on the horizon and began swimming steadily (luckily, I was a very strong swimmer and had been selected for the trials for the 1940 Olympics in the breaststroke).

It must have been late in the afternoon and I was getting tired and losing hope. Several big swells lifted me up and down and I looked all around time and time again. Then I saw behind me and to my left some very small objects. I turned back and began swimming for them. It was a bloody miracle. It was the boats and all the junk. The first thing I grabbed onto was the oak card table, which we had played cards on many times. Then I heard a cry and swam in the direction of a raft (there were two rafts that had popped up when the ship sank). Climbed aboard and it was the first officer, Frits de Jong, lying on the raft with a bullet wound in his head. Broke open the raft locker and put sulphur powder on the wound and bandaged him up. He said they shot him at close range and threw him overboard. About twenty minutes later, P. Spuybroek, the third engineer officer, swam up and that made three. We decided to paddle the raft over to the lifeboat with the radio in it. We then rowed the boat over to a bigger lifeboat and transferred all the food and water from the other boats and the radio into the biggest boat. Carried de Jong into the boat and made him comfortable. The boats were all full of water, as they had not been in the water for many months. As it was going dark by this time, we then began to wrestle up the mast and pull up the sail. We heard another cry and rowed over in the direction of the sound. We picked up Dekker, the second officer, and a lascar, K. Dhange. Dekker had a sword wound in the head, the Lascar was OK.

As soon as it was dark, we set sail for Ceylon, approximately 1,000 miles north of us. Dekker had a compass from the boat, and we propped him up and he steered. The boat kept filling with water and we had to bail all night. By morning, I was sick and lay down for several hours (I guess it all caught up with me). Anyhow, after dozing for several hours I felt better, and we got the boat in shipshape.

De Jong was in a bad way. We decided to wait until the third day before I climbed the mast and rigged the antenna, so I could send a message on the transmitter at night (signals travel further at night). We opened up a can of peaches and had a little extra water and sat down to wait for dark.

It must have been about 6.00 p.m. when we were shelled by a big gun from somewhere. That was my lowest point. I thought, here, after going through all this, the Japs had returned to finish us off. The vessel firing got bigger, and I could see it was a ship. I still thought it was an enemy ship as the shelling continued. Then the ship got bigger and turned a little and I could see it was an American Liberty ship. They came alongside, stopped, and picked us up. It was the SS *James A. Wilder*, out of San Francisco, en route to Calcutta, India. This was the highest moment of my life.

We were treated like a million dollars, and clothed by the crew and showered, and fed like kings.

We landed two days later in Colombo, Ceylon. The wounded went to the hospital and I stayed with an English couple until I managed to get a ticket on a train up through India to Bombay, where I finally got passage on the SS *Strathaird* to Scotland, and leave.

We were interrogated in Ceylon by Lord Louis Mountbatten, who was Commander-in-Chief of the South-East Asia Command. A flying boat went out and located the drifting lifeboats and wood etc. They found no one else.

Each of the five survivors escaped, to the best of my knowledge, as follows:

First off was First Officer Frits de Jong, 6' 6", 280lb, soon after we got underway. Led behind conning tower and shot in the head and pushed overboard. He is still alive and well in Holland. Lives in Texel [Netherlands].

Next was Second Officer Jan Dekker. Led behind conning tower. Attacked with sword and hammer. Knocked overboard and shot at.

Third off was Third Engineer P.F. Spuybroek. Clubbed and knocked overboard.

I was next, with Fourth Officer C. Visser, and I have written how that happened.

The last of the survivors was the British Indian seaman (lascar). He said that after the Japanese had killed most of the prisoners they tied up about twenty of the last who remained and fastened the rope to the sub. All went below and they dived. He was the last man on the end of the human chain and was underwater and going down, when he also got out of the rope around his wrists. He popped up to the surface and had a longer swim than I did. I have never heard from him or what happened afterwards.

In April 1986, James Blears had written to Gus Britton, Assistant Director of the Submarine Museum in Gosport:

I was serving on the SS *Tjisalak* of the Java China Japan Line, a Dutch freighter sailing for the Allies in WWII as second radio officer. Most Allied foreign-flag ships carried at least one British radio officer for the decoding and English messages etc. I had been on the ship around a year all over the world moving stuff around. We left Melbourne, Australia, in March 1944, sailing unescorted with war supplies for Calcutta and the Burma War front.

We were carrying forty lascar survivors from a previous torpedoing, two Australian Army officers who were commandos and were going to India to teach commando tactics to the Indian Army, and an American Red Cross nurse. She was going to Calcutta to join her British officer husband who was in India. The rest were British Navy gunners, about twelve, I think. Two British radio officers, and the chief was Dutch.

To cut a long story short, we were taken on board the sub and Captain Hen and the girl, chief radio officer and chief engineer were taken below in the conning tower. At the War Crimes Trial, a crewmember of *I-8* gave evidence for the Allies. He said they interrogated the ones who were taken below. They took the American girl on deck that night and shot her. How's this one? The lascar told how after I had gone overboard they tied the remainder of the survivors together on a long rope and submerged, towing a human chain of men underwater.

When a lot of the Japanese subs surrendered, their crews had snapshots of many of the atrocities with them, and to this day, I cannot figure this out. Did they think it was OK? We will never know.

On 5 June 1944, I gave my statement to the British Admiralty in London.

Medals were awarded by Queen Wilhelmina of the Netherlands. I got the Kruis Van Verdienste for aiding and saving the lives of the survivors after escaping from the sub and reaching the raft after hours of swimming. It was about five to six hours I swam.

In 1947, I received an invitation to Tokyo to give evidence at the War Crimes Trials there, but I was booked for many wrestling matches and making good money, so I received a bunch of photos etc., and was asked to identify, if I could, some of the Japanese crew of *I-8*.

In the War Crimes Trials, the incident was known as the 'Ichioka Case', as Vice Admiral Hisao Ichioka was in command of Subron 8 Indian Ocean. Jan 1949, he received twenty years' hard labour.

Vice Admiral Teruhisa Komatsu, Commander 6th Fleet, fifteen years' hard labour.

Rear Admiral Noboru Ishizaki, ten years.

Rear Admiral Hisashi Iura, six years.

Officers of the *I-8* at time of my incident were:

Lt. Sadao Motonaka, seven years.

Lt. Masanori Hattori, five years.

ALL SENTENCES WERE COMMUTED AFTER SERVING SIX YEARS.

Albert Kelder, a marine researcher in the Netherlands, supplied the following:

> The *Tjisalak* (5,787 GRT), one of the oldest ships of JCJL (brought into service at the end of the Second World War) had left the Netherlands East Indies from Soerabaja before the surrender. The vessel went to Southampton via an African port and would sail the seas in a rather lucky way. During the heavy air raids on Southampton, she did not get one scratch and sailed unescorted from Gibraltar to Durban, Lourenço Marques and the Persian Gulf. Next, to Trinidad and New York, always on her own and without any mishaps to the ship. In New York, the ancient armament was replaced by a modern 10.2cm gun and machine guns. After that, the *Tjisalak* for some time took part in convoys in the North Atlantic, most of the time loaded with ammunition and explosives. Though observing many ships going down, the '*T*' always remained saved as through a miracle. 'The voyages were a horror,' we read in a report of Chief Officer Frits de Jong, from which we quote some sentences:
>
>> Nobody escaped from the torpedoed ship carrying explosives, and of the other ships people froze to death immediately after falling in the water; the percentage of people saved was minimal. The sailing was almost unbearable, and we sailed on trip after trip.

After some time, the '*T*' had to sail from the UK again for the Persian Gulf via the Mediterranean, also a risky voyage with the old ship, which deep in our hearts we did love, though in fact she is much too slow for our liking.

En route we heard that the sister ship *Tjilboet* had been torpedoed and exploded without any survivors. Some trips had to be made with troops to Bombay, Calcutta and Colombo, always without an escort. In the beginning of 1944, the '*T*' was sent from Colombo to Melbourne with passengers and a full cargo, but sailing alone. In Melbourne, the crew was given the opportunity for a couple of weeks to recover. On 7 March 1944, the *Tjisalak* left for Colombo under the command of Captain C. Hen for what was going to be her last voyage.

Not surprisingly, James Blears left the sea after his eventful voyage in the *Tjisalak*. He settled in the USA and became a successful professional wrestler. In 1955, he moved to Hawaii and founded the Pacific Wrestling Federation, of which he became president. After retiring from the ring, in his words, 'I have spent my time surfing and diving and travelling and doing TV narration sports, and booking wrestlers in Japan etc.'

Just rewards, perhaps?

Epilogue

The final chapter serves as a fitting epitaph for this book. Written by the self-styled 'Lord' James Blears, sometime Olympic athlete, radio officer, professional wrestler, it illustrates the sheer brutality of the Second World War on the high seas.

Not all sinkings were accompanied by such bestiality, but for the merchant seaman unwittingly cast into the thick of the fray, it was a pretty nasty business, nevertheless. To be rudely awakened in the dead of night – and it was usually the dead of night – by the crash of an enemy torpedo, followed by an eerie silence as the ship staggered like a wounded beast, was frightening enough. Then came the desperate scramble to get the boats away, inevitably in complete darkness as the generators would have failed. If they were lucky, and the weather was reasonable – and nine times out of ten, it was blowing a howling gale – they cleared the sinking ship without further casualties, but what of the long days ahead?

In open lifeboats, exposed to the cruellest of the elements, and on a starvation diet, it is not surprising that wartime records show more men died of exposure than were killed directly by the enemy. Those who made it to the shore, or were rescued at sea, were the lucky ones, but the memories of their ordeal would haunt them to their dying day.

Glossary

12-POUNDER	Dual-purpose HA/LA gun of 3-inch calibre, widely used by merchant ships.
AB	Able Seaman. Certificated rank on deck.
ABAFT	Behind, in relation to something on board ship.
ABEAM	At right angles to the fore and aft line of a ship.
AFTERPEAK	Ballast or fresh water tank at stern of ship.
AMIDSHIPS	The middle part of the ship.
ASTERN	Behind the ship.
BEAM	Width of vessel at her widest part.
BINNACLE	Pedestal on which ship's compass is mounted.
BOATSWAIN	Senior deck petty officer. Usually abbreviated to bosun.
BULKHEAD	Steel or wooden division between two compartments.
CLUTTER	Interference on radar caused by rough sea, rain etc.
COAMING	Steel parapet around hatchway.
CORVETTE	Naval vessel of about 900 tons specifically designed and built for convoy escort duties.
DEMS	(Defensively Equipped Merchant Ships) Usually refers to Royal Navy and Royal

Artillery men manning guns aboard merchant ships.

DERRICK | Boom used for loading and discharge of cargo.

DOLDRUMS | Area of light winds and calms near the equator.

DONKEYMAN | Senior engine room rating.

DOUBLE BOTTOM | Space between bottom of ship's hull and watertight floor of holds. Used to carry oil fuel or ballast.

ETA | Estimated time of arrival.

FATHOM | 6 feet or 1.82 metres.

FINE (on bow) | Up to about 5 degrees of arc.

FIREMAN | Engine room rating.

FORECASTLE | (Also fo'c'sle) Space below deck in bows of ship used for crew accommodation or stores.

FORECASTLE HEAD | Deck above forecastle.

FOREPEAK | Ballast or fresh water tank in bows of ship.

FREEBOARD | Distance from main deck to waterline.

GALE FORCE | Force 8. Wind speed 34–40 knots.

GUNWALE | Point where the hull joins the weather deck.

HATCHBOARD | Portable wooden cover for hatchway.

HATCHWAY | Opening in deck giving access to cargo hold.

HOTCHKISS | Light machine gun (.303 calibre) of French design, widely used in merchant ships.

IN BALLAST | Having no cargo on board.

KNOT | A unit of speed equal to one nautical mile per hour, a nautical mile being

	6,080 feet, or the length of one minute of latitude at the Equator.
LEE	The sheltered side.
LIFEBOAT FALLS	Ropes and blocks used with davits for lowering and hoisting a lifeboat.
MAIN DECK	The principal deck of a vessel having more than one deck.
MASTER	One who commands a merchant ship.
MAYDAY	Distress codeword used on radio telephone meaning, 'I require immediate assistance'.
OERLIKON	A 20mm cannon fitted to most Allied merchantmen for defence against air attack.
ORDINARY SEAMAN	Uncertificated seaman with at least twelve months' sea service.
POINT (of compass)	11¼ degrees of arc.
POOP DECK	Raised deck at after end of ship.
PORT	Left-hand side of ship when facing forward.
QUARTER	That part of a ship that is halfway between the beam and the stern.
SCUPPER	Drain at ship's side and in holds to carry away excess water.
SLOOP	Small naval vessel used mainly as convoy escort.
STARBOARD	Right-hand side of ship when facing forward.
STEERAGE WAY	The minimum speed at which a ship's rudder will have effect.
STOKEHOLD	Compartment in engine room of steamer containing boilers and furnaces.
STORM FORCE	Force 10. Wind speed 48–55 knots.
TRIMMER	Engine room rating.
TWEEN DECK	Usually the first deck below main deck.

Index